Workshop on Reordering for Statistical Machine Translation

Held at the 24th International Conference on Computational Linguistics (COLING 2012)

Mumbai, India
9 December 2012

Editors:

Karthik Visweswariah
Ananthakrishnan Ramanathan
Mitesh M. Khapra

ISBN: 978-1-62748-359-9

Printed from e-media with permission by:

Curran Associates, Inc.
57 Morehouse Lane
Red Hook, NY 12571

CURRAN ASSOCIATES INC. proceedings.com

Some format issues inherent in the e-media version may also appear in this print version.

Printed by Curran Associates, Inc. (2013)

For permission requests, please contact the Association for Computational Linguistics at the address below.

Association for Computational Linguistics
209 N. Eighth Street
Stroudsburg, Pennsylvania 18360

Phone: 1-570-476-8006
Fax: 1-570-476-0860

acl@aclweb.org

Additional copies of this publication are available from:

Curran Associates, Inc.
57 Morehouse Lane
Red Hook, NY 12571 USA
Phone: 845-758-0400
Fax: 845-758-2634
Email: curran@proceedings.com
Web: www.proceedings.com

Preface

Statistical Machine Translation (SMT) is currently a very active area of research. Top NLP conferences typically include many papers on SMT, and the past decade has also seen many workshops on this topic (e.g., WMT, SSST). Results reported in papers on SMT include the influence of various components and processes, one of the most important of these being reordering (except for structurally similar language pairs like English-French). Traditional phrase-based SMT systems, which have been the state-of-the-art in the previous decade, do not handle reordering in a satisfactory manner, and various new and more sophisticated methods for reordering have been introduced in the past couple of years. However, unlike most other potential components of MT systems, such as transliteration, WSD, and anaphora resolution, reordering has not had a dedicated forum for its evaluation. The proposed workshop will be a platform to bring together different MT systems and compare how they tackle this crucial subtask.

A shared task on "learning reordering from word-alignments" will be at the heart of this workshop. Parser-based reordering has been a popular method, but many languages do not have parsers (e.g., no Indian language has a publicly available parser), and using alignments to learn parsers (and thereafter reordering) or to learn reordering models directly is an important new idea in MT. The task is to develop a system for reordering a source sentence to best match the order of the corresponding target sentence. For example, the English (SVO language) sentence "Ram drinks water" is translated into Hindi (SOV language) as "Ram paanii piitaa hai (Ram water drinks)". Thus, the correct reordering of this English sentence which matches the target (Hindi) order is "Ram water drinks".

We released high-quality word-alignments (annotated by hand) between English and 3 languages (Farsi, Italian and Urdu), and described one or two baseline techniques for reordering based on publicly available tools (such as GIZA++, Moses). We also made available part-of-speech tags for this data to enable participants to experiment with these additional features easily. The participants have to reorder the English sentences to match the order of the target language. Participants can choose either to come up with their own reordering models or tweak the baseline system to improve performance.

Workshop Chairs

Mitesh M. Khapra, IBM Research India
Ananthakrishnan Ramanathan, IBM Research India
Karthik Visweswariah, IBM Research India

Workshop chairs:
Karthik Visweswariah, Ananthakrishnan Ramanathan and Mitesh M. Khapra

Organizers:

Mitesh M. Khapra (IBM Research India)
Ananthakrishnan Ramanathan (IBM Research India)
Karthik Visweswariah (IBM Research India)

Program Committee:

Abe Ittycheriah (IBM Watson Research Lab)
John DeNero (Google)
Pushpak Bhattacharyya (IIT Bombay)
Philipp Koehn (University of Edinburgh)
Phil Blunsom (Oxford University)

Diamond sponsors

Tata Consultancy Services
Linguistic Data Consortium for Indian Languages (LDC-IL)

Gold Sponsors

Microsoft Research
Beijing Baidu Netcon Science Technology Co. Ltd.

Silver sponsors

IBM, India Private Limited
Crimson Interactive Pvt. Ltd.
Yahoo
Easy Transcription & Software Pvt. Ltd.

Table of Contents

Workshop on Reordering for Statistical Machine Translation

Program

Sunday, 9 December 2012

14:30–15:30	**Invited talk:** *A survey of reordering for MT with a focus on pre-ordeing* Karthik Visweswariah, IBM Research India
15:30–15:40	Introduction to the shared task *Whitepaper for Shared Task on Learning Reordering from Word Alignments at RSMT 2012* *Report of the Shared Task on Learning Reordering from Word Alignments at RSMT 2012*
15:40–16:10	*A Tagging-style Reordering Model for Phrase-based SMT* Minwei Feng and Hermann Ney
16:10–16:30	*Building a reordering system using tree-to-string hierarchical model* Jacob Dlougach and Irina Galinskaya
16:30–17:00	Tea break
17:00–17:20	*Learning Improved Reordering Models for Urdu, Farsi and Italian using SMT* Rohit Gupta, Raj Nath Patel and Ritesh Shah
17:20–17:40	*Partially modelling word reordering as a sequence labelling problem* Anoop Kunchukuttan and Pushpak Bhattacharyya
17:40–18:00	Concluding remarks by workshop chairs

Whitepaper for Shared Task on Learning Reordering from Word Alignments at RSMT 2012

Mitesh M. Khapra[1] *Ananthakrishnan Ramanathan*[1]
Karthik Visweswariah[1]
(1) IBM Research India
{mikhapra,aramana5,v-karthik}@in.ibm.com

Abstract

Several studies have shown that the task of reordering source sentences to match the target order is crucial to improve the performance of Statistical Machine Translation, especially when the source and target languages have significantly divergent grammatical structures. In fact, it is now become a standard practice to include reordering as a pre-processing step or as an integrated module (within the decoder). However, despite the importance of this sub-task, there is no forum dedicated for its evaluation. The objective of the proposed Shared Task is to provide a common benchmarking platform to evaluate state of the art approaches for reordering.

Keywords: Reordering, Machine Translation.

Proceedings of the Workshop on Reordering for Statistical Machine Translation, pages 1–8,
COLING 2012, Mumbai, December 2012.

1 Task Description

The task is to develop a reordering engine to reorder source English sentences to match the order of the target language. For example, the English (SVO language) sentence "Ram drinks water" is translated into Hindi (SOV language) as "Ram paanii piitaa hai (Ram water drinks)". Thus, the correct reordering of this English sentence which matches the target (Hindi) order is "Ram water drinks". The task organizers will release high-quality word-alignments (annotated by hand) between English and 3 languages (*viz.*, Urdu, Farsi and Italian). The participants can use this training and development data to develop a reordering engine for the mentioned source target language pairs. At evaluation time, a list of source sentences will be provided on which the participants will have to run their systems and submit the best reordering for each sentence as output by their system. For every language pair, the participants must submit at least one run which uses only the data provided by the task organizers. This will be called a "standard" run. Participants can submit more than one standard run. In addition, participants can also submit several "non-standard" runs for each language pair which use data other than that provided by the task organizers. The task organizers **will** differentiate between "standard" and "non-standard" runs while preparing the task report.

2 Important Dates

Research Paper Submission Deadline	08-Oct-2012 (23:59 PST)
Shared task	
Release Training/Development Data	10-Sep-2012
Release Test Data	04-Oct-2012
Results Submission Due	08-Oct-2012 (23:59 PST)
Results Announcement	10-Oct-2012
Task (short) Papers Due	15-Oct-2012
For All Submissions	
Acceptance Notification	01-Nov-2012
Camera-Ready Copy Deadline	10-Nov-2012 (23:59 PST)
Workshop Date	09-Dec-2012 (14:00 IST)

3 Data

Participants can register for the task by sending a mail to mikhapra@in.ibm.com and specifying the language pairs that they are interested in. The requested data containing the following files will be then mailed to the participants.

src_tgt.src.[trn|dev].conll : This file is in the standard CoNLL-X format with one word per line and a blank line separating two sentences. Some of the columns have been redefined to suit the reordering task. The columns are as follows:

1. Original index: The index of the word in the original unreordered source sentence
2. word : The lexical form of the word
3. empty : dummy column
4. CPOSTAG: Coarse-grained part-of-speech tag (tagset depends on the language)
5. POSTAG: Fine-grained part-of-speech tag (tagset depends on the language)
6. empty: dummy column

7. Previous Index: The index of the word which precedes this word in the reordered source sentence
8. empty : dummy column
9. empty : dummy column
10. empty : dummy column

Note that the words in the source sentence which do not align to any word in the target sentence will be dropped from the conll file. For example, if the source sentence is "I am going home" and if the word "a" is not aligned to any word in the target sentence then this word will be dropped from the conll file as shown below:

1	I	-	P	PRP	-	0	-	-	-
2	going	-	V	VBG	-	3	-	-	-
3	home	-	N	NOUN	-	1	-	-	-

src_trn.src.[trn|dev].txt : This file contains the complete source sentence (including words which were left unaligned) Example: I am going home.

src_trn.src.[trn|dev].pos : This file contains the pos tags for the complete source sentence (including words which were left unaligned). Example: VRB (I) VMZ (am) VBG (going) NN (home).

src_trn.src.[trn|dev].parse : This file contains a parse for the complete source sentence (including words which were left unaligned). The parse was generated by a state-of-the-art in-house parser.

src_trn.src.[trn|dev].align.info : This file contains indices of only those words which were aligned to some word in the target sentence. Example: 0(I) 2(going) 3 (home)

Note that src_tgt.src.[trn|dev].conll starts at index 1 whereas src_trn.src.[trn|dev].align.info starts at index 0. The participants can use src_tgt.src.[trn|dev].conll and src_trn.src.[trn|dev].align.info to find the words which were left unaligned.

3.1 Language pairs

Table 1 lists the language pairs that will be included in the Shared Task and the amount of hand aligned data that will be released for each language pair (**En**: English, **Fa**: Farsi, **Ur**: Urdu, **It**: Italian).

Language Pair	Train	Dev	Test
En-Fa	5K	500	500
En-Ur	5K	500	500
En-It	4K	500	500

Table 1: Language Pairs included in the Shared Task

3.2 Terms of usage

By requesting for the data the participants agree to the following:

1. using the dataset only for research purposes and not for any non-research/commercial purposes
2. submitting at least one run for the requested language pair
3. submitting a short paper describing their approach/system

Also note that the participants cannot redistribute the dataset in part or in whole nor can they republish it on any other site.

4 Submissions

At evaluation time, participants will be provided with test data containing the 4 files (conll, txt, pos, parse) described above. One "standard" run must be submitted by each group for each language pair. Additional "standard" runs (upto 4 in total can also be submitted). The best of the submitted "standard" runs will be used for reporting performance summary. In addition to "standard" runs the participants can also submit upto 4 "non-standard" runs. The results must be submitted in CoNLL-X format with the 7th column containing the previous index for each word as predicted by the participants system. There should be one conll file for every run. All the conll files should be zipped into a single zip file and mailed to mikhapra@in.ibm.com. The "standard" and "non-standard" runs must be labeled clearly.

4.1 Short Papers on Task

Each participating group is required to submit a short paper describing their approach. Participants should follow COLING 2012 paper submission policy including paper format, blind review policy and title and author format convention. The task paper should be a short paper containing 8 A5 sized pages with any number of reference pages.

5 Evaluation Metrics

The output reorderings will be evaluated using two metrics:

- **BLEU** (Papineni et al., 2001): In the past decade, BLEU has been the most widely used metric for MT evaluation. BLEU compares N-grams in the output translation and the reference translation(s), and uses a "brevity penalty" to prevent outputs that are accurate in terms of N-gram match, but too short.

  For reordering, we use the BLEU metric by comparing candidate reorderings with the reference reorderings that we create from the hand-alignments.

  BLEU is calculated as:

$$log(BLEU) = min(1 - \frac{r}{c}, 0) + \sum_{n=1}^{N} \frac{1}{N} log(p_n)$$

$$\begin{aligned} where, N &= 4 (unigrams,\ bigrams,\ trigrams,\ and\ 4\text{-}grams\ are\ matched) \\ r &= length\ of\ reference\ reordering \\ c &= length\ of\ candidate\ reordering \end{aligned}$$

  and

$$p_n = \frac{\sum_{C \in Candidates} \sum_{n\text{-}gram \in C} Count_{clip}(n\text{-}gram)}{\sum_{C \in Candidates} \sum_{n\text{-}gram \in C} Count_{clip}(n\text{-}gram)}$$

where C runs over the entire set of candidate reorderings, and $Count_{clip}$ returns the number of n-grams that match in the reference reordering.

- **LRscore** (Birch and Osborne, 2010):

  LRscore was introduced a couple of years ago as a metric to directly measure reordering performance. LRscore uses a distance score in conjunction with BLEU to help evaluate the word order of MT outputs better. Experiments show that this combined metric correlates better with human judgments than BLEU alone (Birch and Osborne, 2010). Since we do not need a lexical metric, we use only the distance metric from LRscore. We will evaluate reordering distance using the following two scores:

  - Hamming distance: This measures the number of disagreements between two permutations:

$$d_H(\pi, \rho) = 1 - \frac{\sum_{i=1}^{n} x_i}{n}, \text{ where } x_i = \begin{cases} 0 & \text{if } \pi(i) = \rho(i), \\ 1 & \text{otherwise,} \end{cases}$$

  - Kendall's Tau Distance: This measures the minimum number of transpositions of two adjacent symbols necessary to transform one permutation into another:

$$d_r(\pi, \rho) = 1 - \frac{\sum_{i=1}^{n} \sum_{j=1}^{n} z_{ij}}{Z}, \text{ where } z_{ij} = \begin{cases} 1 & \text{if } \pi(i) < \pi(j) \text{ and } \rho(i) > \rho(j) \\ 0 & \text{otherwise} \end{cases}$$

$$Z = \frac{(n^2 - n)}{2}$$

  These two distance metrics will be combined with a brevity penalty (as defined in the description of BLEU above).

Links to these evaluation scripts are provided on the workshop webpage[1].

6 Baseline

The baseline score will be obtained by comparing the unreordered source sentence with the reference.

7 Some Pointers

We encourage participation from researchers in other areas such as parsing and language modeling, who may find reordering to be a good application area and extrinsic evaluation of their work. For such participants and others new to the problem of reordering and MT, the following pointers may be useful to get started with the task.

[1] https://sites.google.com/site/rsmt2012/Shared-Task/evaluation-scripts

- **Statistical MT toolkits**: Reordering can be thought of as translation from unreordered to reordered text. Setting up the unreordered text as the source corpus and the reordered text as the target corpus with publicly available MT toolkits like Moses (phrase-based MT toolkit: www.statmt.org/moses/), Hiero and Joshua could be a simple starting point for the task. We have observed improvements using Moses with the above setup, using the default settings, and only the target reordered corpus as the LM data. It should be possible to improve further with better features. For example, we could use a POS factor and a POS LM, or we could do some morphological processing to work with the roots and suffixes. It may also be important to tune various parameters, such as the distortion model parameters, which may be quite sensitive to the language pair.
- **Parser-based reordering**: If the source-language has a parser (we provide parses for the input sentences for the shared task), a few rules could be written for reordering (Collins et al., 2005) or rules could be automatically learnt based on the alignments (Visweswariah et al., 2010).
- **Reordering without a parser**: Some recent work has focussed on reordering without a parser. Examples are the word reordering models in Visweswariah et al. (2011) and Tromble et al. (2009). DeNero and Uszkoreit (2011) describe a technique to induce parse trees from alignments, and use these parses for reordering.

8 Contact Us

Name	Email
Mitesh M. Khapra	mikhapra@in.ibm.com
Ananthakrishnan Ramanathan	aramana5@in.ibm.com
Karthik Visweswariah	v-karthik@in.ibm.com

References

Birch, A. and Osborne, M., (2010). LRScore for evaluating lexical and reordering quality in MT. *Proceedings of the Fifth Workshop on Statistical Machine Translation.*

Collins, M., Koehn, P., and Kučerová, I. (2005). Clause restructuring for statistical machine translation. In *Proceedings of ACL*, pages 531–540, Morristown, NJ, USA. Association for Computational Linguistics.

DeNero, J. and Uszkoreit, J. (2011). Inducing sentence structure from parallel corpora for reordering. In *Proceedings of the Conference on Empirical Methods in Natural Language Processing*, EMNLP '11, pages 193–203, Stroudsburg, PA, USA. Association for Computational Linguistics.

Papineni, K., Roukos, S., Ward, T., and Zhu, W., (2001). BLEU: a method for automatic evaluation of machine translation. *IBM Research Report*, Thomas J. Watson Research Center.

Tromble, R., and Eisner, J., (2009). Learning linear ordering problems for better translation. In *Proceedings of EMNLP.*

Visweswariah, K., Navratil, J., Sorensen, J., Chenthamarakshan, V., and Kambhatla, N. (2010). Syntax based reordering with automatically derived rules for improved statistical machine translation. In *Proceedings of the 23rd International Conference on Computational Linguistics*.

Visweswariah, K., Rajkumar, R., Gandhe, A., Ramanathan, A., and Navratil, J., (2011). A word reordering model for improved machine translation. In *Proceedings of the Conference on Empirical Methods in Natural Language Processing*, EMNLP '11, pages 486–496, Stroudsburg, PA, USA. Association for Computational Linguistics.

Report of the Shared Task on Learning Reordering from Word Alignments at RSMT 2012

Mitesh M. Khapra[1] *Ananthakrishnan Ramanathan*[1]
Karthik Visweswariah[1]
(1) IBM Research India
{mikhapra,aramana5,v-karthik}@in.ibm.com

Abstract
Several studies have shown that the task of reordering source sentences to match the target order is crucial to improve the performance of Statistical Machine Translation, especially when the source and target languages have significantly divergent grammatical structures. In fact, it is now become a standard practice to include reordering as a pre-processing step or as an integrated module (within the decoder). However, despite the importance of this sub-task, there is no forum dedicated for its evaluation. The objective of this Shared Task was to provide a common benchmarking platform to evaluate state of the art approaches for reordering.

Keywords: Reordering, Machine Translation.

Proceedings of the Workshop on Reordering for Statistical Machine Translation, pages 9–16,
COLING 2012, Mumbai, December 2012.

1 Task Description

The task was to develop a reordering engine to reorder source English sentences to match the order of the target language. For example, the English (SVO language) sentence "Ram drinks water" is translated into Hindi (SOV language) as "Ram paanii piitaa hai (Ram water drinks)". Thus, the correct reordering of this English sentence which matches the target (Hindi) order is "Ram water drinks". The task organizers released high-quality word-alignments (annotated by hand) between English and 3 languages (*viz.*, Urdu, Farsi and Italian). The participants used this training and development data to develop a reordering engine for the mentioned source target language pairs. At evaluation time, a list of source sentences was provided on which the participants had to run their systems and submit the best reordering for each sentence as output by their system. For every language pair, the participants were supposed to submit at least one run which uses only the data provided by the task organizers. This was called a "standard" run. Participants were allowed to submit more than one standard run. In addition, participants were also allowed to submit several "non-standard" runs for each language pair which use data other than that provided by the task organizers.

2 Data

The following data files were provided to the participants for each language pair.

src_tgt.src.[trn|dev].conll : This file is in the standard CoNLL-X format with one word per line and a blank line separating two sentences. Some of the columns have been redefined to suit the reordering task. The columns are as follows:

1. Original index: The index of the word in the original unreordered source sentence
2. word : The lexical form of the word
3. empty : dummy column
4. CPOSTAG: Coarse-grained part-of-speech tag (tagset depends on the language).
5. POSTAG: Fine-grained part-of-speech tag (tagset depends on the language).
6. empty: dummy column
7. Previous Index: The index of the word which precedes this word in the reordered source sentence
8. empty : dummy column
9. empty : dummy column
10. empty : dummy column

Note that the words in the source sentence which do not align to any word in the target sentence will be dropped from the conll file. For example, if the source sentence is "I am going home" and if the word "a" is not aligned to any word in the target sentence then this word will be dropped from the conll file as shown below:

1	I	-	P	PRP	-	0	-	-	-
2	going	-	V	VBG	-	3	-	-	-
3	home	-	N	NOUN	-	1	-	-	-

src_trn.src.[trn|dev].txt : This file contains the complete source sentence (including words which were left unaligned). Example: I am going home.

src_trn.src.[trn|dev].pos : This file contains the pos tags for the complete source sentence (including words which were left unaligned). Example: VRB(I) VMZ(am) VBG(going) NN(home).

src_trn.src.[trn|dev].parse : This file contains a parse for the complete source sentence (including words which were left unaligned). The parse was generated by a state-of-the-art in-house parser.

src_trn.src.[trn|dev].align.info : This file contains indices of only those words which were aligned to some word in the target sentence. Example: 0(I) 2(going) 3 (home)

Note that src_tgt.src.[trn|dev].conll starts at index 1 whereas src_trn.src.[trn|dev].align.info starts at index 0. The participants can use src_tgt.src.[trn|dev].conll and src_trn.src.[trn|dev].align.info to find the words which were left unaligned.

2.1 Language pairs

Table 1 lists the language pairs that were included in the Shared Task and the amount of hand aligned data that was released for each language pair (**En**: English, **Fa**: Farsi, **Ur**: Urdu, **It**: Italian). **This data which was released as a part of the shared task can be obtained by sending a mail to mikhapra@in.ibm.com**.

Language Pair	Train	Dev	Test
En-Fa	5K	500	500
En-Ur	5K	500	500
En-It	4K	500	500

Table 1: Language Pairs included in the Shared Task

3 Evaluation Metrics

The output reorderings were evaluated using two metrics:

- **BLEU** (Papineni et al., 2002): In the past decade, BLEU has been the most widely used metric for MT evaluation. BLEU compares N-grams in the output translation and the reference translation(s), and uses a "brevity penalty" to prevent outputs that are accurate in terms of N-gram match, but too short.

  For reordering, we use the BLEU metric by comparing candidate reorderings with the reference reorderings that we create from the hand-alignments.

  BLEU is calculated as:

$$log(BLEU) = min(1 - \frac{r}{c}, 0) + \sum_{n=1}^{N} \frac{1}{N} log(p_n)$$

$$where, N = 4 (unigrams,\ bigrams,\ trigrams,\ and\ 4\text{-}grams\ are\ matched)$$
$$r = length\ of\ reference\ reordering$$
$$c = length\ of\ candidate\ reordering$$

and

$$p_n = \frac{\sum_{C \in Candidates} \sum_{n\text{-}gram \in C} Count_{clip}(n\text{-}gram)}{\sum_{C \in Candidates} \sum_{n\text{-}gram \in C} Count_{clip}(n\text{-}gram)}$$

where C runs over the entire set of candidate reorderings, and $Count_{clip}$ returns the number of n-grams that match in the reference reordering.

- **LRscore** (Birch and Osborne, 2010):

  LRscore was introduced a couple of years ago as a metric to directly measure reordering performance. LRscore uses a distance score in conjunction with BLEU to help evaluate the word order of MT outputs better. Experiments show that this combined metric correlates better with human judgments than BLEU alone (Birch and Osborne, 2010). Since we do not need a lexical metric, we use only the distance metric from LRscore. We will evaluate reordering distance using the following two scores:

  - Hamming distance: This measures the number of disagreements between two permutations:

$$d_H(\pi, \rho) = 1 - \frac{\sum_{i=1}^{n} x_i}{n}, \text{ where } x_i = \begin{cases} 0 & \text{if } \pi(i) = \rho(i), \\ 1 & \text{otherwise,} \end{cases}$$

  - Kendall's Tau Distance: This measures the minimum number of transpositions of two adjacent symbols necessary to transform one permutation into another:

$$d_r(\pi, \rho) = 1 - \frac{\sum_{i=1}^{n} \sum_{j=1}^{n} z_{ij}}{Z}, \text{ where } z_{ij} = \begin{cases} 1 & \text{if } \pi(i) < \pi(j) \text{ and } \rho(i) > \rho(j) \\ 0 & \text{otherwise} \end{cases}$$

$$Z = \frac{(n^2 - n)}{2}$$

  These two distance metrics will be combined with a brevity penalty (as defined in the description of BLEU above).

Links to these evaluation scripts are provided on the workshop webpage[1].

4 Systems

Seven groups requested for the data released in the Shared Task. However, eventually only 3 groups made a clean submission. In this section, we briefly describe the systems submitted by these three groups.

Gupta et al. (2012) treated reordering as translation from unreordered to reordered text. They used a publicly available phrase-based MT toolkit (Moses[2]) for learning this translation model by setting up the unreordered text as the source corpus and the reordered text as

[1]https://sites.google.com/site/rsmt2012/Shared-Task/evaluation-scripts
[2] www.statmt.org/moses/

the target corpus. They experimented with both, a phrase based model and a factor based model. The phrase based model was trained without any preprocessing or reordering of data. The factored based model used 'surface word form' and the 'POS tag' factors as translation-factors for training. The map value <0-0,1> was provided in the training script which indicated a source side (surface) to a target side (surface, POS) mapping. They experimented with different values of distortion-limit and used default settings for all other parameters (for both translation model and language model).

Kunchukuttan and Bhattacharyya (2012) model the problem of reordering source sentences as a problem of reordering word sequences (as opposed to reordering words). They consider source side reordering to be a composition of the following operations on a sentence: (1) Breaking the sentence into word sequences (2) Reversing the words within some word sequences and (3) Reordering the word sequences. They model the first two steps as a sequence labeling problem. The labeling scheme captures word sequence boundaries and reversals, and the training data labels are extracted using the word alignment information provided by the task organizers. The third step is modeled as a Traveling Salesperson (TSP) problem. They consider word sequences, instead of words, to be the cities, and define the cost of traveling from one city to another. The costs are assigned so that the total cost will be minimum for the correct reordering of word sequences. The costs are computed as a function of features of the word sequences involved, and a regression based cost model is learned. The use of word sequences makes solving the TSP problem more tractable, and helps define relevant word-sequence level features for modeling the cost.

Dlougach and Galinskaya (2012) built a syntax-based reordering system using on open-source SMT toolkit (Moses). Using source side parses and word alignment information they learn reordering rules from the small corpus provided by the task organizers. They then apply these rules to reorder the test sentences. They claim that this approach works especially well when source and target languages have different sentence-level order (like Subject-Verb-Object vs. Subject-Object-Verb). Its also accounts for word-level reordering (when nouns are swapped with their corresponding adjectives). While working on this shared task they have also made changes to the source code of Moses, especially its chart decoder. These changes are available in the public repository of Moses (Dlougach and Galinskaya, 2012).

5 Results

As mentioned earlier, the different systems that participated in the Shared Task were evaluated using mBLEU (Table 2), $LR_{Hamming}$ (Table 3) and $LR_{Kendall}$ (Table 4) . To put the results in perspective we compare these systems with a baseline system (which uses no reordering) and a state of the art system which models reordering as a Traveling Salesman Problem (Visweswariah et al., 2011). Note that Visweswariah et al. (2011) did not participate in the Shared Task. Their results are included only for the sake of comparison.

6 Summary and future possibilities

We conducted a Shared Task on Learning Reordering from Word Alignments. The participants were supposed to train reordering models using high quality alignment data as well as pos tagged and parsed source sentences. We provided data for three language pairs (*viz.*, En-Farsi, En-Urdu and En-Italian). A total of seven groups requested for this data but eventually only three groups made a clean submission. These three systems were evaluated

System	En-Fa	En-It	En-Ur
	mBLEU	mBLEU	mBLEU
Baseline	50.0	65.1	38.3
Dlougach and Galinskaya (2012)	65.6	76.7	55.8
Gupta et al. (2012)	55.7	73.0	44.7
Kunchukuttan and Bhattacharyya (2012)	46.4	64.7	37.8
Visweswariah et al. (2011)	68.7	83.0	63.3

Table 2: mBLEU scores of different systems that participated in the Shared Task.

System	En-Fa	En-It	En-Ur
	$LR_{Hamming}$	$LR_{Hamming}$	$LR_{Hamming}$
Baseline	0.418	0.707	0.268
Dlougach and Galinskaya (2012)	0.549	0.771	0.428
Gupta et al. (2012)	0.432	0.751	0.313
Kunchukuttan and Bhattacharyya (2012)	0.086	0.283	0.112
Visweswariah et al. (2011)	0.576	0.817	0.507

Table 3: $LR_{Hamming}$ scores of different systems that participated in the Shared Task.

System	En-Fa	En-It	En-Ur
	$LR_{Kendall}$	$LR_{Kendall}$	$LR_{Kendall}$
Baseline	0.716	0.858	0.491
Dlougach and Galinskaya (2012)	0.748	0.875	0.592
Gupta et al. (2012)	0.712	0.867	0.510
Kunchukuttan and Bhattacharyya (2012)	0.349	0.529	0.348
Visweswariah et al. (2011)	0.764	0.894	0.643

Table 4: $LR_{Kendall}$ scores of different systems that participated in the Shared Task.

using 2 metrics: mBLEU and LR score. Two out of the three participants were able to get reasonable gains over the baseline system (which uses no reordering). The enthusiasm shown for the first offering of this Shared Task was encouraging and we plan to organize this Shared Task again. In the next offering of the Shared Task, we would like to see the performance in the other direction *i.e.* non-English to English.

References

Birch, A. and Osborne, M. (2010). Lrscore for evaluating lexical and reordering quality in mt. In *Proceedings of the Joint Fifth Workshop on Statistical Machine Translation and MetricsMATR*, WMT '10, pages 327–332, Stroudsburg, PA, USA. Association for Computational Linguistics.

Dlougach, J. and Galinskaya, I. (2012). Building a reordering system using tree-to-string hierarchical model. In *Proceedings of the First Workshop on Reordering for Statistical Machine Translation at COLING 2012*, Mumbai, India.

Gupta, R., Patel, R. N., and Shah, R. (2012). Some experiments: Reordering using aligned bilingual corpus. In *Proceedings of the First Workshop on Reordering for Statistical Machine Translation at COLING 2012*, Mumbai, India.

Kunchukuttan, A. and Bhattacharyya, P. (2012). Partially modelling word reordering as a sequence labelling problem. In *Proceedings of the First Workshop on Reordering for Statistical Machine Translation at COLING 2012*, Mumbai, India.

Papineni, K., Roukos, S., Ward, T., and Zhu, W.-J. (2002). Bleu: a method for automatic evaluation of machine translation. In *Proceedings of the 40th Annual Meeting on Association for Computational Linguistics*, ACL '02, pages 311–318, Stroudsburg, PA, USA. Association for Computational Linguistics.

Visweswariah, K., Rajkumar, R., Gandhe, A., Ramanathan, A., and Navratil, J. (2011). A word reordering model for improved machine translation. In *Proceedings of the Conference on Empirical Methods in Natural Language Processing*, EMNLP '11, pages 486–496, Stroudsburg, PA, USA. Association for Computational Linguistics.

A Tagging-style Reordering Model for Phrase-based SMT

Minwei FENG Hermann NEY
Human Language Technology and Pattern Recognition Group,
Computer Science Department,
RWTH Aachen University,
Aachen, Germany
`feng@cs.rwth-aachen.de`, `ney@cs.rwth-aachen.de`

ABSTRACT
For current statistical machine translation system, reordering is still a major problem for language pairs like Chinese-English, where the source and target language have significant word order differences. In this paper we propose a novel tagging-style reordering model. Our model converts the reordering problem into a sequence labeling problem, i.e. a tagging task. For the given source sentence, we assign each source token a label which contains the reordering information for that token. We also design an unaligned word tag so that the unaligned word phenomenon is automatically covered in the proposed model. Our reordering model is conditioned on the whole source sentence. Hence it is able to catch long dependencies in the source sentence. The decoder makes use of the tagging information as soft constraints so that in the test phase (during translation) our model is very efficient. The model training on large scale tasks requests notably amounts of computational resources. We carried out experiments on five Chinese-English NIST tasks trained with BOLT data. Results show that our model improves the baseline system by 0.98 BLEU 1.21 TER on average.

KEYWORDS: statistical machine translation, reordering, conditional random fields.

Proceedings of the Workshop on Reordering for Statistical Machine Translation, pages 17–26,
COLING 2012, Mumbai, December 2012.

1 Introduction

The systematic word order difference between two languages pose a challenge for current statistical machine translation (SMT) systems. The system has to decide in which order to translate the given source words. This problem is known as the reordering problem. As shown in (Knight, 1999), if arbitrary reordering is allowed, the search problem is NP-hard.

In this paper, we propose a novel tagging style reordering model. Our model converts the reordering problem into a sequence labeling problem, i.e. a tagging task. For a given source sentence, we assign each source token a label which contains the reordering information for that token. We also design an unaligned word tag so that the unaligned word phenomenon is automatically covered in the proposed model. Our model is conditioned on the whole source sentence. Hence it is able to capture the long dependencies in the source sentence. We choose the conditional random fields (CRFs) approach for the tagging model. Although utilizing CRFs on large scale task requests a notable amount of computational resources, the decoder makes use of the tagging information as soft constraints. Therefore, the training procedure of our model is computationally expensive while in the test phase (during translation) our model is very efficient.

The remainder of this paper is organized as follows: Section 2 reviews the related work for solving the reordering problem. Section 3 introduces the basement of this research: the principle of statistical machine translation. Section 4 describes the proposed model. Section 5 provides the experimental configuration and results. Conclusion will be given in Section 6.

2 Related Work

Many ideas have been proposed to address the reordering problem. Within the phrase-based SMT framework there are mainly three stages where improved reordering could be integrated:

1. Reorder the source sentence. So that the word order of source and target sentences is similar. Usually it is done as the preprocessing step for both training data and test data.
2. In the decoder, add models in the log-linear framework or constraints in the decoder to reward good reordering options or penalize bad ones.
3. In the reranking framework.

For the first point, (Wang et al., 2007) used manually designed rules to reorder parse trees of the source sentences as a preprocessing step. Based on shallow syntax, (Zhang et al., 2007) used rules to reorder the source sentences on the chunk level and provide a source-reordering lattice instead of a single reordered source sentence as input to the SMT system. Designing rules to reorder the source sentence is conceptually clear and usually easy to implement. In this way, syntax information can be incorporated into phrase-based SMT systems. However, one disadvantage is that the reliability of the rules is often language pair dependent.

In the second category, researchers try to inform the decoder on what a good reordering is or what a suitable decoding sequence is. (Zens and Ney, 2006) used a discriminative reordering model to predict the orientation of the next phrase given the previous phrase. (Mariño et al., 2006) presents a translation model that constitutes a language model of a sort of "bilanguage" composed of bilingual units. From the reordering point of view, the idea is that the correct reordering is to find the suitable order of translation units. (Cherry, 2008) puts the syntactic cohesion as a soft constraint in the decoder to guide the decoding process to choose those translations that do not violate the syntactic structure of the source sentence. Adding new features in the log-linear framework has the advantage that the new feature has access to the whole search space. Another advantage of methods in this category is that we let the decoder decide the weights of features, so that even if one model gives wrong estimation sometimes, it can still be corrected by other models. Our work in this paper belongs to this category.

In the reranking step, the system has the last opportunity to choose a good translation. (Och et al., 2004) describe the use of syntactic features in the rescoring step. They report the most useful feature is IBM Model 1 score. The syntactic features contribute very small gains. Another disadvantage of carrying out reordering in reranking is the representativeness of the N-best list is often a question mark.

3 Translation System Overview

In this section, we are going to describe the phrase-based SMT system we used for the experiments. In statistical machine translation, we are given a source language sentence $f_1^J = f_1 \ldots f_j \ldots f_J$. The objective is to translate the source into a target language sentence $e_1^I = e_1 \ldots e_i \ldots e_I$. The strategy is among all possible target language sentences, we will choose the one with the highest probability:

$$\hat{e}_i^{\hat{I}} = \arg\max_{I, e_1^I} \{ Pr(e_1^I | f_1^J) \} \tag{1}$$

We model $Pr(e_1^I|f_1^J)$ directly using a log-linear combination of several models (Och and Ney, 2002):

$$Pr(e_1^I|f_1^J) = \frac{\exp\left(\sum_{m=1}^{M} \lambda_m h_m(e_1^I, f_1^J) \right)}{\sum_{I', e'^{I'}_1} \exp\left(\sum_{m=1}^{M} \lambda_m h_m(e'^{I'}_1, f_1^J) \right)} \tag{2}$$

The denominator is to make the $Pr(e_1^I|f_1^J)$ to be a probability distribution and it depends only on the source sentence f_1^J. For search, the decision rule is simply:

$$\hat{e}_i^{\hat{I}} = \arg\max_{I, e_1^I} \left\{ \sum_{m=1}^{M} \lambda_m h_m(e_1^I, f_1^J) \right\} \tag{3}$$

The model scaling factors λ_1^M are trained with Minimum Error Rate Training (MERT).

In this paper, the phrase-based machine translation system is utilized (Och et al., 1999; Zens et al., 2002; Koehn et al., 2003). The translation process consists in segmenting of the source sentence according to the phrase table which is built from the word alignment. The translation of each of these segments consists just in extracting the target side from the phrase pair. With the corresponding target side, the final translation is the composition of these translated segments. In this last step, reordering is allowed.

4 Tagging-style Reordering Model

In this section, we describe the proposed model. First we will describe the training process. Then we explain how to use the model in the decoder.

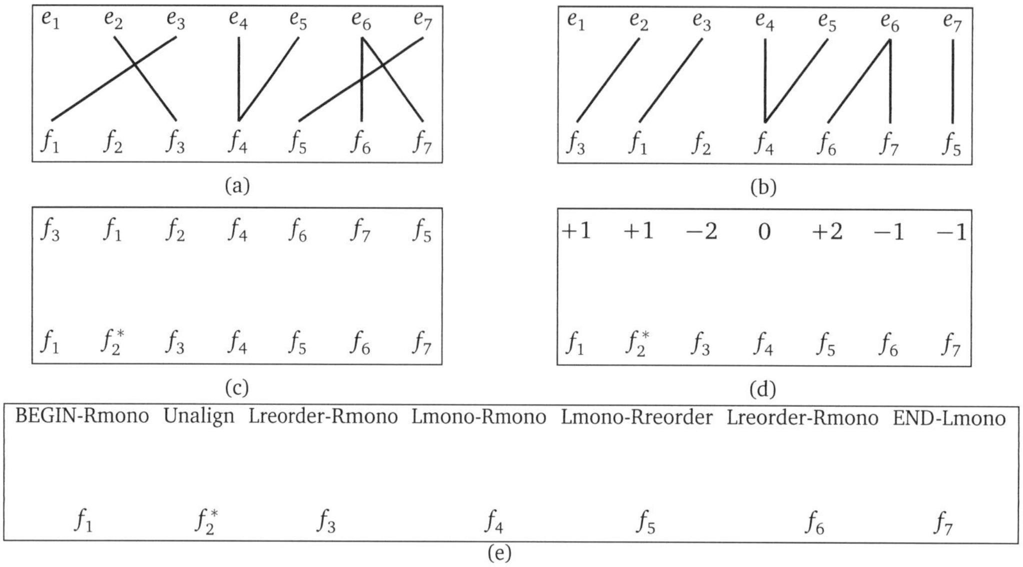

Figure 1: Modeling process illustration.

4.1 Modeling

Figure 1 demonstrates the modeling steps. The first step is word alignment training. Figure 1(a) is an example after GIZA++ training. If we regard this alignment as a translation result, i.e. given the source sentence f_1^7, the system translates it into the target sentence e_1^7. The alignment link set $\{a_1 = 3, a_3 = 2, a_4 = 4, a_4 = 5, a_5 = 7, a_6 = 6, a_7 = 6\}$ reveals the decoding process, i.e. the alignment implies the order in which the source words should be translated, e.g. the first generated target word e_1 has no alignment, we can regard it as a translation from a NULL source word; then the second generated target word e_2 is translated from f_3. We reorder the source side of the alignment to get Figure 1(b). Figure 1(b) implies the source sentence decoding sequence information, which is depicted in Figure 1(c). Using this example we describe the strategies we used for special cases in the transformation from Figure 1(b) to Figure 1(c):

- ignore the unaligned target word, e.g. e_1
- the unaligned source word should follow its preceding word, the unaligned feature is kept with a $*$ symbol, e.g. f_2^* is after f_1
- when one source word is aligned to multiple target words, only keep the alignment that links the source word to the first target word, e.g. f_4 is linked to e_5 and e_6, only $f_4 - e_5$ is kept. In other words, every source word appears only once in the source decoding sequence.
- when multiple source words are aligned to one target word, put together the source words according to their original relative positions, e.g. e_6 is linked to f_6 and f_7. So in the decoding sequence, f_6 is before f_7.

Now Figure 1(c) shows the original source sentence and its decoding sequence. By using the strategies above, it is guaranteed that the source sentence and its decoding sequence has the exactly same length. Hence the relation can be modeled by a function $F(f)$ which assigns a value for each of the source word f. Figure 1(d) manifests this function. The positive function values mean that compared to the original position in the source sentence, its position in the decoding sequence should move right, and vice versa. If the function value is 0, the word's position in original source sentence and its decoding sequence is same. For example, f_1 is the first word in the source sentence but it is the second word in the decoding sequence. So its function value is +1 (move right one position).

Now Figure 1(d) converts the reordering problem into a sequence labeling or tagging problem. To move the computational cost to a reasonable level, we do a final simplification step in Figure 1(e). Suppose the longest sentence length is 100, then according to Figure 1(d), there are 200 tags (from -99 to +99 plus the unalign tag). As we will see later, this number is too large for our task. We instead design nine tags. For a source word f_j in one source sentence f_1^J, the tag of f_j will be one of the following:

BEGIN-Rmono $j = 1$ and f_{j+1} is translated *after* f_j (Rmono for right monotonic)

BEGIN-Rreorder $j = 1$ and f_{j+1} is translated *before* f_j (Rreorder for right reordered)

END-Lmono $j = J$ and f_{j-1} translated *before* f_j (Lmono for left monotonic)

END-Lreorder $j = J$ and f_{j-1} translated *after* f_j (Lreorder for left reordered)

Lmono-Rmono $1 < j < J$ and f_{j-1} translated *before* f_j and f_j translated *before* f_{j+1}

Lmono-Rreorder $1 < j < J$ and f_{j-1} translated *before* f_j and f_j translated *after* f_{j+1}

Lreorder-Rmono $1 < j < J$ and f_{j-1} translated *after* f_j and f_j translated *before* f_{j+1}

Lreorder-Rreorder $1 < j < J$ and f_{j-1} translated *after* f_j and f_j translated *after* f_{j+1}

Unalign f_j is an unaligned source word

Up to this point, we have converted the reordering problem into a tagging problem with nine tags. The transformation in Figure 1 is conducted for all the sentence pairs in the bilingual training corpus. After that, we have built an "annotated" corpus for the training. For this supervised structure learning task, we choose the approach conditional random fields (CRFs) (Lafferty et al., 2001; Sutton and Mccallum, 2006; Lavergne et al., 2010). More specifically, we adopt the linear-chain CRFs. However, even for the simple linear-chain CRFs, the complexity of learning and inference grows quadratically with respect to the number of output labels and the amount of structural features which are with regard to adjacent pairs of labels. Hence, to make the computational cost as low as possible, two measures have been taken. Firstly, as described above we reduce the number of tags to nine. Secondly, we add source sentence part-of-speech (POS) tags to the input. For features with window size one to three, both source words and its POS tags are used. For features with window size four and five, only POS tags are used.

4.2 Decoding

Once the CRFs training is finished, we make inference on develop and test corpora. After that we get the labels of the source sentences that need to be translated. In the decoder, we add a new model which checks the labeling consistence when scoring an extended state. During the search, a sentence pair (f_1^J, e_1^I) will be formally splitted into a segmentation S_1^K which consists of K phrase pairs. Each $s_k = (i_k; b_k, j_k)$ is a triple consisting of the last position i_k of the kth target phrase $\tilde{e}_k$. The start and end position of the kth source phrase $\tilde{f}_k$ are b_k and j_k. Suppose the search state is now extended with a new phrase pair $(\tilde{f}_k, \tilde{e}_k)$:

$$\tilde{f}_k := f_{b_k} \dots f_{j_k} \tag{4}$$

$$\tilde{e}_k := e_{i_{k-1}+1} \dots e_{i_k} \quad (5)$$

We have access to the old coverage vector, from which we know if the left neighboring source word f_{b_k-1} and the right neighboring source word f_{j_k+1} of the new phrase have been translated. We also have the word alignment within the new phrase pair, which is stored during the phrase extraction process. Based on the old coverage vector and alignment, we can repeat the transformation in Figure 1 to calculate the labels for the new phrase. The added model will then check the consistence between the calculated labels and the labels predicted by the CRFs. The number of source words that have inconsistent labels is regarded as penalty and then the penalty is added as a new feature into the log-linear framework.

5 Experiments

In this section, we describe the baseline setup, the CRFs training results and translation experimental results.

5.1 Experimental Setup

Our baseline is a phrase-based decoder, which includes the following models: an n-gram target-side language model (LM), a phrase translation model and a word-based lexicon model. The latter two models are used for both directions: $p(f|e)$ and $p(e|f)$. Additionally we use phrase count features, word and phrase penalty. The reordering model for the baseline system is the distance-based jump model which uses linear distance. This model does not have hard limit. We list the important information regarding the experimental setup below. All those conditions have been kept same in this work.

- lowercased training data (Table 1) from the BOLT task
  alignment trained with GIZA++
- development corpus: NIST06 test corpora: NIST02 03 04 05 and 08
- 5-gram LM (1 694 412 027 running words) trained by SRILM toolkit (Stolcke, 2002) with modified Kneser-Ney smoothing
  training data: target side of bilingual data.
- BLEU (Papineni et al., 2001) and TER (Snover et al., 2005) reported
  all scores calculated in lowercase way.
- Wapiti toolkit (Lavergne et al., 2010) used for CRFs

	Chinese	**English**
Sentences	5 384 856	
Running Words	115 172 748	129 820 318
Vocabulary	1 125 437	739 251

Table 1: training data statistics

5.2 CRFs Training Results

Table 1 contains the data statistics used for translation model and LM. For the reordering model, we take two further filtering steps. Firstly, we delete the sentence pairs if the source sentence length is one. When the source sentence has only one word, the translation will be always monotonic and the reordering model does not need to learn this. Secondly, we delete the sentence pairs if the source sentence contains more than three contiguous unaligned words.

When this happens, the sentence pair is usually low quality hence not suitable for learning. The main purpose of the two filtering steps is to further lay down the computational burden. We then divide the corpus into three parts: train, validation and test. The source side data statistics for CRFs training is given in Table 2 (target side has only 9 labels). The toolkit Wapiti

	train	validation	test
Sentences	2 973 519	400 000	400 000
Running Words	62 263 295	8 370 361	8 382 086
Vocabulary	454 951	149686	150 007

Table 2: reordering model training data statistics

(Lavergne et al., 2010) is used in this paper. We choose the classical optimization algorithm limited memory BFGS (L-BFGS) (Liu and Nocedal, 1989). For regularization, Wapiti uses both the ℓ^1 and ℓ^2 penalty terms, yielding the elastic-net penalty of the form

$$\rho_1 \cdot \parallel \theta \parallel_1 + \frac{\rho_2}{2} \cdot \parallel \theta \parallel_2^2 \tag{6}$$

In this work, we use as many features as possible because ℓ^1 penalty $\rho_1 \parallel \theta \parallel_1$ is able to yield sparse parameter vectors, i.e. using a ℓ^1 penalty term implicitly performs the feature selection. On a cluster with two AMD Opteron(tm) Processor 6176 (total 24 cores), the training time is about 16 hours, peak memory is around 120G. Several experiments have been done to find the suitable hyperparameters ρ_1 and ρ_2. We choose the model with lowest error rate on the validation corpus for the translation experiments. The error rate of the chosen model on test corpus is 25.75% for token error rate and 69.39% for sequence error rate. The error rate values are much higher than what we usually see in part-of-speech tagging task. The main reason is that the "annotated" corpus is converted from word alignment which contains a lot of errors. However, as we will show later, the learned CRFs model helps to improve the translation quality. The feature template we set initially will generate 722 999 637 features. After training 36 902 363 features are kept.

5.3 Translation Results

Results are summarized in Table 3. Automatic measure BLEU and TER scores are provided. Also we report significance testing results on both BLEU and TER. We perform bootstrap resampling with bounds estimation as described in (Koehn, 2004). We use the 95% confidence threshold (denoted by ‡ in the table) to draw significance conclusions. Besides the five test corpora, we add a column **avg.** to show the average improvements. We also add a column **Index** for score reference convenience.

From Table 3 we see that our proposed reordering model is able to improve the baseline by 0.98 BLEU and 1.21 TER on average. The largest BLEU improvement 1.11 is from NIST04 and the largest TER improvement 1.57 is from NIST03. For line 2 and 6, the significance test was done and most scores are better than their corresponding baseline values with more than 95% confidence (scores marked with ‡).

We also compare our model with the widely used Moses Lexicalized Reordering Model (Koehn et al., 2007). Line 3 and 7 are the results. Results show that for BLEU both model achieve almost same results (average improvement 0.98 BLEU versus 0.99 BLEU). For TER, our tagging-style reordering model is 0.25 points better (average improvement 1.21 TER versus 0.96 TER). When

Systems	NIST02	NIST03	NIST04	NIST05	NIST08	avg.	Index
			BLEU scores				
baseline	33.60	34.29	35.73	32.15	26.34	-	1
baseline+CRFs	34.53	35.19	36.56‡	33.30‡	27.41‡	0.98	2
baseline+Moses	34.87	34.90	36.40	33.43	27.45	0.99	3
baseline+CRFs+Moses	35.41	35.63	37.24	33.98	27.47	1.52	4
			TER scores				
baseline	61.36	60.48	59.12	60.94	65.17	-	5
baseline+CRFs	60.14‡	58.91‡	57.91‡	59.77‡	64.30‡	1.21	6
baseline+Moses	60.07	59.08	58.42	59.74	64.50	0.96	7
baseline+CRFs+Moses	59.33	58.48	57.44	59.12	64.43	1.65	8

Table 3: Experimental results

the tagging-style reordering model is used together with the lexicalized reordering model, further improvements have been observed. Results are presented in line 4 and 8. The two models improve the baseline by 1.52 BLEU and 1.65 TER on average.

6 Conclusion

In this paper, a novel tagging style reordering model has been proposed. By our modeling method, the reordering problem is converted into a sequence labeling problem so that the whole source sentence is taken into consideration for the reordering decisions. By adding an unaligned word tag, the unaligned word phenomenon is automatically covered in the proposed model. Although the training phase of our model is computationally expensive, its usage for decoding is quite simple. In practice, this algorithm does not significantly increase memory or computation requirements during decoding.

We choose CRFs to accomplish the relational learning task. The learning task needs 120G memory and lasts for 16 hours. Both ℓ^1 and ℓ^2 penalty are used in regularization. Hence the feature selection is automatically conducted. For test corpus, the token error rate is 25.75% and sequence error rate is 69.39%.

We utilize the CRFs model as soft constraints in the decoder. Experimental results show that our model is stable and improves the baseline system by 0.98 BLEU and 1.21 TER. Most of the scores are better than their corresponding baseline values with more than 95% confidence.

The comparison with Moses Lexicalized Reordering Model has been done. Results show that our model achieve the same performance with the lexicalized reordering model on BLEU measure. For TER the tagging-style reordering model is 0.25 points better. By applying the tagging-style reordering model and lexicalized reordering model together, further improvements can be achieved. The lexicalized reordering model only captures the dependency between neighboring phrases while our model uses the whole source sentence information.

7 Acknowledgements

This work was supported by the Defense Advanced Research Projects Agency (DARPA) under Contract No. 4911028154.0. Any opinions, findings and conclusions or recommendations expressed in this material are those of the authors and do not necessarily reflect the views of the Defense Advanced Research Projects Agency (DARPA).

References

Cherry, C. (2008). Cohesive phrase-based decoding for statistical machine translation. In *Proceedings of ACL-08: HLT*, pages 72–80, Columbus, Ohio.

Knight, K. (1999). Decoding complexity in word-replacement translation models. *Comput. Linguist.*, 25(4):607–615.

Koehn, P. (2004). Statistical significance tests for machine translation evaluation. In *Proceedings of EMNLP*, pages 388–395, Barcelona, Spain.

Koehn, P., Hoang, H., Birch, A., Callison-Burch, C., Federico, M., Bertoldi, N., Cowan, B., Shen, W., Moran, C., Zens, R., Dyer, C., Bojar, O., Constantin, A., and Herbst, E. (2007). Moses: open source toolkit for statistical machine translation. In *Proceedings of the 45th Annual Meeting of the ACL on Interactive Poster and Demonstration Sessions*, ACL '07, pages 177–180, Stroudsburg, PA, USA. Association for Computational Linguistics.

Koehn, P., Och, F. J., and Marcu, D. (2003). Statistical phrase-based translation. In *Proceedings of the 2003 Conference of the North American Chapter of the Association for Computational Linguistics on Human Language Technology - Volume 1*, NAACL '03, pages 48–54, Stroudsburg, PA, USA. Association for Computational Linguistics.

Lafferty, J. D., McCallum, A., and Pereira, F. C. N. (2001). Conditional random fields: Probabilistic models for segmenting and labeling sequence data. In *Proceedings of the Eighteenth International Conference on Machine Learning*, ICML '01, pages 282–289, San Francisco, CA, USA. Morgan Kaufmann Publishers Inc.

Lavergne, T., Cappé, O., and Yvon, F. (2010). Practical very large scale CRFs. In *Proceedings the 48th Annual Meeting of the Association for Computational Linguistics (ACL)*, pages 504–513. Association for Computational Linguistics.

Liu, D. C. and Nocedal, J. (1989). On the limited memory bfgs method for large scale optimization. *Math. Program.*, 45(3):503–528.

Mariño, J. B., Banchs, R. E., Crego, J. M., de Gispert, A., Lambert, P., Fonollosa, J. A. R., and Costa-Jussà, M. R. (2006). *N*-gram-based machine translation. *Computational Linguistics*, 32(4):527–549.

Och, F. J., Gildea, D., Khudanpur, S., Sarkar, A., Yamada, K., Fraser, A., Kumar, S., Shen, L., Smith, D., Eng, K., Jain, V., Jin, Z., and Radev, D. (2004). A smorgasbord of features for statistical machine translation. In *Proceedings of NAACL-HLT-04*, pages 161–168, Boston, Massachusetts, USA.

Och, F. J. and Ney, H. (2002). Discriminative training and maximum entropy models for statistical machine translation. In *Proceedings of ACL-02*, pages 295–302, Philadelphia, Pennsylvania, USA.

Och, F. J., Tillmann, C., and Ney, H. (1999). Improved alignment models for statistical machine translation. In *Proc. of the Joint SIGDAT Conf. on Empirical Methods in Natural Language Processing and Very Large Corpora (EMNLP99)*, pages 20–28, University of Maryland, College Park, MD, USA.

Papineni, K., Roukos, S., Ward, T., and Zhu, W.-J. (2001). Bleu: a method for automatic evaluation of machine translation. (RC22176 (W0109-022)).

Snover, M., Dorr, B., Schwartz, R., Makhoul, J., Micciulla, L., and Weischedel, R. (2005). A study of translation error rate with targeted human annotation. Technical Report LAMP-TR-126, CS-TR-4755, UMIACS-TR-2005-58, University of Maryland, College Park, MD.

Stolcke, A. (2002). Srilm - an extensible language modeling toolkit. In *Proceedings of ICSLP-02*, pages 901–904, Denver, Colorado,USA.

Sutton, C. and Mccallum, A. (2006). *Introduction to Conditional Random Fields for Relational Learning*. MIT Press.

Wang, C., Collins, M., and Koehn, P. (2007). Chinese syntactic reordering for statistical machine translation. In *Proceedings of the EMNLP/CoNLL-07*, pages 737–745, Prague, Czech Republic.

Zens, R. and Ney, H. (2006). Discriminative reordering models for statistical machine translation. In *Proceedings of the Workshop on Statistical Machine Translation at HLT-NAACL-06*, pages 55–63, New York City, NY.

Zens, R., Och, F. J., and Ney, H. (2002). Phrase-based statistical machine translation. In *German Conference on Artificial Intelligence*, pages 18–32. Springer Verlag.

Zhang, Y., Zens, R., and Ney, H. (2007). Chunk-level reordering of source language sentences with automatically learned rules for statistical machine translation. In *Proceedings of the NAACL-HLT-07/AMTA Workshop on Syntax and Structure in Statistical Translation*, pages 1–8, Morristown, NJ, USA.

Building a reordering system using tree-to-string hierarchical model

Jacob DLOUGACH[1] *Irina GALINSKAYA*[1]
(1) Yandex School of Data Analysis, 16 Leo Tolstoy St., Moscow 119021, Russia
jacob@yandex-team.ru, galinskaya@yandex-team.ru

ABSTRACT

This paper describes our submission to the First Workshop on Reordering for Statistical Machine Translation. We have decided to build a reordering system based on tree-to-string model, using only publicly available tools to accomplish this task. With the provided training data we have built a translation model using Moses toolkit, and then we applied a chart decoder, implemented in Moses, to reorder the sentences. Even though our submission only covered English-Farsi language pair, we believe that the approach itself should work regardless of the choice of the languages, so we have also carried out the experiments for English-Italian and English-Urdu. For these language pairs we have noticed a significant improvement over the baseline in BLEU, Kendall-Tau and Hamming metrics. A detailed description is given, so that everyone can reproduce our results. Also, some possible directions for further improvements are discussed.

KEYWORDS : reordering with parse, tree-to-string model, Moses toolkit

Proceedings of the Workshop on Reordering for Statistical Machine Translation, pages 27–36,
COLING 2012, Mumbai, December 2012.

1 Introduction

As participants of the First Workshop on Reordering for SMT, we were required to build a system to reorder words in a source English sentence in such way, that it would match the order of words in a translation of that sentence into the target language (which could be Farsi, Urdu or Italian in our case).

After receiving the training data, we have noticed many common patterns in the sentences. For example, Farsi turned out to have constituent word order of "subject-object-verb" and noun order of (usually) "noun-modifier", which is different from English "subject-verb-object" and "modifier-noun" respectively. Considering a very small amount of training data (5000 sentences), we have decided that making a lexical-only model would be unreasonable, but such amount can still be enough for building a reliable syntax-based model (Quirk and Corston-Oliver, 2006), so we have decided to build such model with rules being automatically extracted from the training corpus.

2 Model training

2.1 Model description

We have used a model, often referred to as "tree-to-string" (Nguyen et al., 2008) to find the best reordering candidate. In this model some sequences of consecutive words (further referred to as word spans) are assigned syntax labels. These labels could either be syntax entities (like predicate) or part of speech tags. If the labels are induced by a syntax parse, they form a tree structure, i.e. if two labelled spans share common words, then one of them is enclosed inside the other one.

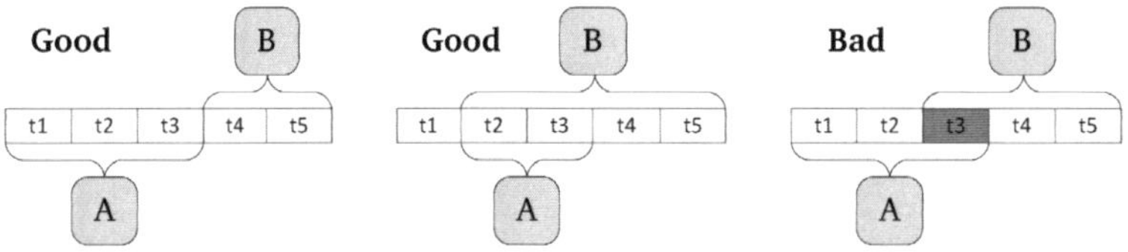

FIGURE 1 – EXAMPLES OF CORRECT AND INCORRECT SPAN LABELLING

For our purposes we can assume, that every word has its own label (i.e. part of speech tag). The model uses an assumption that we may assemble the reordering for the whole sentence from permutations of its syntax blocks (Hwa et al., 2002). More formally, we can describe this process using synchronous context-free grammar (further abbreviated as SCFG) (Chiang, 2007). Let's say that each of the possible labels is matched by a class within the grammar. Then the rules describing expansions of non-terminals will define a reordering *iff* there is a perfect matching between symbols on the source side of the rule and the target side (i.e. matching symbols should strictly coincide). It should be noted, that such expansion can include both terminals (single words) and non-terminals (syntax classes).

2.2 Dropping words

However, in the data that we have been provided with, some words from the source sentences may have been dropped and, thus, there were no words from the target sentences matching them. At this point, we have found two ways of adjusting the initial model to account for this peculiarity of the data. One possible approach is to remove some words after the reordering without changing the model itself. Another approach is to allow certain deletions inside the rules. Since we have had an "a priori" knowledge about the words that are to be dropped, we can enable the decoder to use this knowledge, so that the language model can estimate translation hypotheses become more precisely. We have assumed that only the syntax properties of dropped words matter for reordering of the rest of the sentence, so we have simply substituted these words with a special symbol that is guaranteed not to occur anywhere else in the data sets. The second approach has demonstrated significantly better performance on the development set, so we have decided not to include the results of the first one into our final submission.

2.3 Data preparation

The training set required some pre-processing for Moses to read it. We needed to convert the parse file into XML format accepted by Moses and also to provide the alignments between source and target sentences. The alignments have been derived directly from the data, whereas the XML was obtained from the parse escaping all special symbols and then applying the following substitution rules:

[{class}	**<tree label="**{class}**">**
{class}**]**	**</tree>**
{word}_{pos}	**<tree label="**{pos}**">** {word} **</tree>**

TABLE 1 – SUBSTITUTION RULES FOR PROCESSING THE PARSE

2.4 Training steps

Moses training pipeline consists of nine steps:

1. Prepare data
2. Run GIZA++
3. Align words
4. Get lexical translation table
5. Extract phrases
6. Score phrases
7. Build lexicalized reordering model
8. Build generation models
9. Create configuration file

In our case the data have been prepared separately and the alignments were given explicitly, so it was not required for us to run the first three steps. Also since we are training a hierarchical model, step 7 (lexicalized reordering model) is not applicable, and since we know exact translations of each word, it isn't reasonable to build a generation model either. Therefore we are only left with steps 4-6 and 9. It is worth noting, though, that step 4 can be done separately as well, because single words are always left unchanged during the translation process (except for special symbol standing for dropped words), and step 9 isn't really configurable, so further we will only focus on extraction and scoring of the rules.

2.4.1 Extraction

Extraction has been carried out using an *extract-rules* tool in Moses. Since default parameters in this tool are tuned assuming phrase-based translation, we have needed some adjustments. Here is the list of used non-default parameters:

Parameter	Value	Comments
`GlueGrammar`	N/A	This parameter enables creation of rules to glue any two spans together without changing their order. When no rules can be applied, this one will always guarantee that at least one translation will be produced.
`MinHoleSource`	1	Default value is 2, which is good for hierarchical models, but too strict for syntax models.
`MaxSymbolsSource`	4	Greater values have proved to slow down the process of rule extraction and scoring too much.
`MaxSpan`	999	This means that we can extract rules spanned over the whole sentence.
`MaxNonTerm`	4	Default is 2, and we actually want to generate rules where all symbols could be non-terminals.
`NonTermConsecSource`	N/A	This allows two non-terminals on source side to appear adjacent to each other.
`MinWords`	0	This specifies the minimum number of terminals. Reasons for selection of this value are the same as in MaxNonTerm parameter.

TABLE 2 – *EXTRACT* TOOL CONFIGURATION

Here are some examples of the extracted rules:

Source phrase	Target phrase	Alignment
`[ADJP][X] [NN][X] [NP]`	`[NN][X] [ADJP][X] [X]`	`1-0 0-1`
`having political [NNS][X] [VP]`	`having [NNS][X] political [X]`	`0-0 2-1 1-2`
`$ [CD][X] billion [QP]`	`[CD][X] billion $ [X]`	`1-0 2-1 0-2`

TABLE 3 – EXAMPLES OF EXTRACTED RULES

2.4.2 Scoring

Rules are then assigned weights using *score* tool. In order to be able to restore the alignment of the target phrase into the source phrase, we have specified "`WordAlignment`" flag (otherwise it would only print alignments of the non-terminals). Also we have decided to utilize Good-Turing frequency estimation (Good, 1953) due to low amount of available parallel sentences and the resulting data sparseness.

2.4.3 Language model

We have decided to build a simple 3-gram language model based on the target sentences as a corpus using IRSTLM toolkit (Federico, Bertoldi and Cettolo, 2008). The necessary steps exactly follow Moses tutorial on building a baseline system (Koehn, 2012). Briefly speaking, we have added sentence boundary symbols and have counted n-grams with Kneser-Ney smoothing (Chen and Goodman, 1996).

3 Decoding

Decoding has been performed using a chart decoder, implemented in Moses. Data preparation has involved building an XML representation of the parse tree, as in section 2.3.

3.1 Printing alignments

At the time we started carrying out the task, alignments output didn't work in the chart decoder: even though the corresponding option could be specified, the decoder would fail at loading time if word alignments were present in the rule table. It turned out that the decoder had relied heavily on the alignments being listed for non-terminals only, so the source code needed some enhancements to lift this restriction.

Then in order to print the alignments for a given translation we have recursively built alignments for each constituting hypothesis. Also we have needed to pay some attention to the unknown words, because the alignments would be explicitly set for them, which is always "0-0" assuming that words in the sentences are zero-indexed.

Since the option to print the alignments in chart decoder was highly demanded by the community, these changes have been integrated into the public Moses repository.

3.2 Decoding parameters

Since we have needed to generate the best possible translations, we have decided to lift most of the constraints in the decoder. Also we have manually added an entry into the rules table in order to delete the words that shouldn't be present in the target sentence (if we are substituting all these words with a special symbol as described in section 2.1). The parameters that we have changed from the default configuration, generated by training pipeline, are listed in Table 4.

Parameter name	Value	Comment
`ttable-limit`	0	Lifts the constraint on number of possible load translations per source phrase in rules table.
`cube-pruning-pop-limit`	100000	Number of top hypotheses to consider for each span.
`max-chart-span`	1000, 1000	Allows each rule to span across literally the whole sentence, thus enabling the decoder to move words from the beginning to the very end of even a long sentence.

TABLE 4 – DECODER CONFIGURATION

4 Tuning

4.1 Technics

We have performed the tuning with the tools coming with Moses: MERT (Och, 2003) and MIRA (Venkatapathy and Joshi, 2007), both using only BLEU score for optimization. The tuned weights have corresponded to one feature in the language model and five features in the translation model (descriptions of each specific feature in the translation model can be found in Moses tutorial). It's worth noting, that the default value of using 100 best translations on each step hasn't been very efficient, because Moses has tended to generate 100 absolutely equal translations of one sentence using different rules and, for some reason, hasn't merged them while decoding, so we have used a limit of 2000. First, we have trained a model with removal of unneeded words after the translation process, and tuned it with MERT. However, when we decided to remove the words during decoding, all suggested metrics (which will be discussed further) have shown an increase of reordering quality on the development set even without any further tuning.

The tuning for the second model was not converging when MERT was used (actually, it seemed to be oscillating heavily), so we have utilized MIRA, which has recently been integrated into Moses. The changes occurring at every iteration have become less dramatic than with MERT, but on the other side number of iterations, required to get some stable result, has increased. The quality actually increased, but only by a small margin.

4.2 Analysis

Three of the features in translation model have been assigned negative weights. Since this is a rather strange event, we have tried to provide some explanation for it. One of those features corresponds to glue rules. Since glue rules actually have positive feature scores, it's pretty reasonable for them to be assigned negative weights, since their usage during translation results in unchanged order regardless of other rules. Another negative weight corresponds to phrase penalty. This means that decoder should attempt to use as few rules as possible, like in phrase-based translation, where using longer phrases would provide more reliable translation. The third weight is inverse phrase translation probability (conditional probability of source phrase provided the target phrase). While this could seem really strange for phrase-based translation, in syntax-based translation models having negative weight assigned to inverse translation probability results in taking additional syntax-based language model as a supplementary feature:

$$P_{final}(f|e) \propto p_{tm}(e|f)^{\lambda_1} \cdot p_{tm}(f|e)^{\lambda_2} \cdot p_{lm}(f)^{\lambda_3} = p_{tm}(e|f)^{\lambda_1+\lambda_2} \cdot \left(\frac{p_{tm}(f)}{p_{tm}(e)}\right)^{\lambda_2} \cdot p_{lm}(f)^{\lambda_3}$$

In this formula p_{tm} stands for probabilities estimated by translation model, while p_{lm} stands for language model approximation. f is the sentence with Farsi word order, and e is the source English sentence. Note that this differs from the notation commonly used in other statistical machine translation works, where f would be source language and e would be target language.

In our case λ_1 is negative, but λ_2 and λ_3 are positive. Moreover, $\lambda_1 + \lambda_2$ is positive too. Notice that $p_{tm}(f)$ is can be treated as another language model, which is syntax-aware. Therefore, we can come to a conclusion, that inverse translation probability actually would be assigned a positive weight if our language model was syntax-based. Also, cumulative weight of the language model is equal to $\lambda_2 + \lambda_3$, which in our case is approximately 1.5 times higher than cumulative weight of the translation model – $\lambda_1 + \lambda_2$. Thus, we can conjecture that having a better language model could considerably increase the quality of our reordering.

5 Evaluation

Model training has been carried out on a 3 sets of 5000 English sentences each (all sets corresponding to different language pairs). Regardless of the target languages we followed exactly the same procedure for model training as described above in section 2. Both development and testing sets have consisted of 500 sentences each. As a baseline we have taken the unaltered word order.

5.1 Metrics

Three metrics have been used for the evaluation: BLEU, Kendall's tau distance, and Hamming distance (Birch and Osborne, 2010). It should be noted though, that the last two are measured in fraction remaining to maximum value (i.e. if distance is 0 the metric would be 1.0, and if distance is maximal possible the metric equals 0.0).

5.2 Results for development set

Model	English – Farsi	English – Italian	English – Urdu
	BLEU (%) / Kendall tau / Hamming		
Baseline	51.29 / 0.761 / 0.435	69.0 / 0.867 / 0.723	39.5 / 0.52 / 0.274
Delete words after translation; tuned with MERT	67.1 / 0.795 / 0.532	N/A	N/A
Delete words during translation; tuned with MERT	69.5 / 0.805 / ***0.567***	N/A	N/A

Model	English – Farsi	English – Italian	English – Urdu
Delete words during translation; tuned with MIRA	***69.8 / 0.807 /0.567***	***78.3 / 0.884 / 0.779***	***55.7 / 0.649 / 0.431***

TABLE 5 – SCORES FOR THE DEVELOPMENT SET

As you can see, although we have only optimized BLEU, all other metrics increase at the same time. The results for different models are only included for English-Farsi because it has been our primary language pair for this shared task, while English-Italian and English-Urdu results have only qualified as post-submission experiments.

5.3 Results for testing set

For the testing set only BLEU scores are known.

Model	English – Farsi	English – Italian	English – Urdu
Baseline	50.0	66.4	39.0
Delete words during translation; tuned with MERT	65.24	N/A	N/A
Delete words during translation; tuned with MIRA	***65.56***	***76.65***	***55.79***

TABLE 6 – SCORES FOR THE TESTING SET

Conclusion and perspectives

We have managed to build a reordering system without any prior knowledge of the target language. The model has been built with Moses training pipeline and then has been applied to the testing data using chart decoder. We could observe a significant increase in all quality metrics comparing to a simple baseline (not reordered sentences).

Under the time constraints of the workshop, we haven't been able to try all of the options, so there are some ways for improvements. First of all it may be worth changing some of the parameters in learning, such as length of generated rules or smoothing options. Another way is to relax syntax constraints to allow more aggressive reordering when the parse tree is very sparse (i.e. some nodes have many children). As far as we could see after manually inspecting errors in our reordering, this will potentially boost the quality of reordering, however it will require some changes in Moses training scripts. Also, our analysis shows, that it may be very useful to utilize a better language model during decoding.

References

Birch, A. and Osborne, M. (2010). LRscore for Evaluating Lexical and Reordering Quality in MT. *Proceedings of the Joint Fifth Workshop on Statistical Machine Translation and MetricsMATR*, Uppsala, Sweden, 327-332.

Chen, S.F. and Goodman, J. (1996). An empirical study of smoothing techniques for language modeling. *Proceedings of the 34th annual meeting on Association for Computational Linguistics*, Stroudsburg, PA, USA, 310-318.

Chiang, D. (2007). Hierarchical Phrase-Based Translation, *Computational Linguistics*, vol. 33, no. 2, June, pp. 201-228, Available: ISSN: 0891-2017 DOI: 10.1162/coli.2007.33.2.201.

Chiang, D., Lopez, A., Madnani, N., Monz, C., Resnik, P. and Subotin, M. (2005). The Hiero Machine Translation System: Extensions, Evaluation, and Analysis. *Proceedings of Human Language Technology Conference and Conference on Empirical Methods in Natural Language Processing*, Vancouver, British Columbia, Canada, 779-786.

Federico, M., Bertoldi, N. and Cettolo, M. (2008). IRSTLM: an open source toolkit for handling large scale language models. *INTERSPEECH*, 1618-1621.

Fox, H. (2002). Phrasal Cohesion and Statistical Machine Translation. *Proceedings of the Conference on Empirical Methods in Natural Language Processing (EMNLP)*, Philadelphia, 304-311.

Good, I.J. (1953). The population frequencies of species and the estimation of population parameters, *Biometrika*, vol. 40(3 and 4), pp. 237-264.

Hoang, H. and Koehn, P. (2008). Design of the moses decoder for statistical machine translation. *Software Engineering, Testing, and Quality Assurance for Natural Language Processing*, Stroudsburg, PA, USA, 58-65.

Hoang, H. and Koehn, P. (2010). Improved translation with source syntax labels. *Proceedings of the Joint Fifth Workshop on Statistical Machine Translation and MetricsMATR*, Stroudsburg, PA, USA, 409-417.

Hoang, H. and Lopez, A. (2009). A unified framework for phrase-based, hierarchical, and syntax-based statistical machine translation. *In Proceedings of the International Workshop on Spoken Language Translation (IWSLT*, 152-159.

Huang, L., Knight, K. and Joshi, A. (2006). Statistical Syntax-Directed Translation with Extended Domain of Locality. *5th Conference of the Association for Machine Translation in the Americas (AMTA)*, Boston, Massachusetts.

Hwa, R., Resnik, P., Weinberg, A. and Kolak, O. (2002). Evaluating Translational Correspondence using Annotation Projection. *Proceedings of the 40th Annual Meeting of the Association of Computational Linguistics (ACL)*.

Koehn, P. (2012). Moses: Statistical Machine Translation System. User Manual and Code Guide. http://www.statmt.org/moses/manual/manual.pdf. Accessed on 1 October 2012.

Koehn, P. and Hoang, H. (2007). Factored Translation Models. *Proceedings of the 2007 Joint Conference on Empirical Methods in Natural Language Processing and Computational Natural Language Learning (EMNLP-CoNLL)*, 868-876.

Koehn, P., Hoang, H., Birch, A., Callison-Burch, C., Federico, M., Bertoldi, N., Cowan, B., Shen, W., Moran, C., Zens, R., Dyer, C.J., Bojar, O., Constantin, A. and Herbst, E. (2007). Moses: Open Source Toolkit for Statistical Machine Translation. *Proceedings of the 45th Annual Meeting of the Association for Computational Linguistics Companion Volume Proceedings of the Demo and Poster Sessions*, Prague, Czech Republic, 177-180.

Li, C.-H., Li, M., Zhang, D., Li, M., Zhou, M. and Guan, Y. (2007). A Probabilistic Approach to Syntax-based Reordering for Statistical Machine Translation. *Proceedings of the 45th Annual Meeting of the Association of Computational Linguistics*, Prague, Czech Republic, 720-727.

Li, C.-H., Zhang, H., Zhang, D., Li, M. and Zhou, M. (2008). An Empirical Study in Source Word Deletion for Phrase-Based Statistical Machine Translation. *Proceedings of the Third Workshop on Statistical Machine Translation*, Columbus, Ohio, 1-8.

Nguyen, T.P., Shimazu, A., Ho, T.B., Nguyen, M.L. and Nguyen, V.V. (2008). A Tree-to-String Phrase-based Model for Statistical Machine Translation. *CoNLL 2008: Proceedings of the Twelfth Conference on Computational Natural Language Learning*, Manchester, England, 143-150.

Och, F.J. (2003). Minimum Error Rate Training in Statistical Machine Translation. *Proceedings of the 41st Annual Meeting of the Association for Computational Linguistics*, 160-167.

Och, F.J. and Ney, H. (2003). A Systematic Comparison of Various Statistical Alignment Models, *Computational Linguistics*, vol. 29, no. 1, pp. 19-52.

Papineni, K., Roukos, S., Ward, T. and Zhu, W.-J. (2001). BLEU: a Method for Automatic Evaluation of Machine Translation. Tech. rep. *IBM Research Report*.

Quirk, C. and Corston-Oliver, S. (2006). The impact of parse quality on syntactically-informed statistical machine translation. *Proceedings of the 2006 Conference on Empirical Methods in Natural Language Processing*, Sydney, Australia, 62-69.

Venkatapathy, S. and Joshi, A.K. (2007). Discriminative word alignment by learning the alignment structure and syntactic divergence between a language pair. *Proceedings of the NAACL-HLT 2007/AMTA Workshop on Syntax and Structure in Statistical Translation*, Stroudsburg, PA, USA, 49-56.

Yamada, K. and Knight, K. (2001). A Syntax-Based Statistical Translation Model. *Proceedings of the 39th Annual Meeting of the Association of Computational Linguistics (ACL)*.

Learning Improved Reordering Models for Urdu, Farsi and Italian using SMT

Rohit GUPTA[1] *Raj Nath PATEL*[1] *Ritesh SHAH*[1]
(1) CDAC Mumbai, Gulmohar Cross Road No. 9, Juhu, Mumbai, India
rohitg@cdac.in, rajnathp@cdac.in, ritesh@cdac.in

ABSTRACT

This paper presents some experiments which have been carried out as part of a shared task for the workshop "Reordering for Statistical Machine Translation" (RSMT, collocated with COLING 2012). The shared task objective is to learn reordering models by making use of a manually word-aligned, bilingual parallel data. We view this task as that of a statistical machine translation (SMT) system which implicitly employ such models. These models are obtained using empirical methods and machine learning techniques. We have therefore used "Moses"; a state of the art SMT system to conduct experiments for the task at hand. The training and the development datasets used for the experiments have been provided by RSMT and we report our work on three pair of languages namely English-Urdu, English- Farsi and English- Italian.

KEYWORDS : reordering, factored, alignment, statistical, SMT, Moses, BLEU, GIZA++, Urdu, Farsi, Persian, Italian

Proceedings of the Workshop on Reordering for Statistical Machine Translation, pages 37–46,
COLING 2012, Mumbai, December 2012.

1 Introduction

The objective of the shared task is to learn reordering models by making use of human-annotated parallel data which is word aligned. We have transformed this task into one of empirical machine translation where model parameters for the system are learnt using parallel training data and machine learning techniques.

A statistical machine translation (SMT) system primarily relies on two models viz. the translation model (TM) and the language model (LM). In essence, it involves learning mutual correspondences using bilingual parallel data and reducing divergences among the source-target language pair. The alignment models which help establish such links, and the reordering models which help reduce the word order differences in the source-target pair constitute a part of the TM and are an implicit part of such an SMT system. Thus, our motivation to use the SMT system for the shared task comes from the alignment model GIZA++ (Och and Ney, 2003) and the basic reordering model (distance based distortion) employed in the Moses (Koehn et al., 2007) framework. Section 2 briefly explains the GIZA++ alignment model and Section 3 elaborates on the reordering model.

Across many language pairs, the existing SMT systems are usually infested with a lack of resources which leads to reduced annotations on the source and/or target side. Use of machine learning techniques, data preprocessing or other heuristics is mostly employed to overcome this lack of information and estimate good translation models. However, the training data provided in this shared task has the necessary alignment information on both sides. Availability of such information initially motivated us to use simple techniques of chunking based on source-target index information thereby modeling large distance word movements. However, we failed in these initial experiments which resulted in even lesser scores than those trained on a phrase based baseline system.

Therefore, the experiments were planned with only a scope of

1. training a baseline phrase based translation model; elaborated in Section 4.
2. training a factored translation model (Koehn and Hoang, 2007) with linguistic annotations as factors; explained in Section 5.

The BLEU (Papineni et al., 2001) score was the evaluation metric chosen to compare various results. The experiments and results are detailed in Section 6, followed by conclusions.

2 Alignment model

GIZA++is an open source toolkit used to train IBM Models 1-5 (Brown et al., 1993) and an HMM word alignment model (Vogel et al., 1996).

Given a source string $s_1^J = s_1, \dots, s_j, \dots, s_J$ and a target string $t_1^I = t_1, \dots, t_i, \dots, t_I$

An alignment A of the two strings is defined as

$$A \subseteq \{(j, i) : j = 1, \dots, J; i = 0, \dots, I\}$$

In statistical word alignment, the probability of a source sentence given target sentence is written as:

$$P(s_1^J|t_1^I) = \sum_{a_1^J} P(s_1^J, a_1^J|t_1^I)$$

where a_1^J denotes the alignment across the sentence pair. Expressing the probability in statistical terms leads to $P(s_1^J, a_1^J|t_1^I) = p_\theta(s_1^J, a_1^J|t_1^I)$

The parameters θ can be estimated using maximum likelihood estimation (MLE) on a training corpus. If a corpus has N sentences

$$\hat{\theta} = \text{argmax}_\theta \prod_{n=1}^{N} \sum_a p_\theta(s_n, a|t_s)$$

The best alignment of a sentence pair is given by

$$\hat{a}_1^J = \text{argmax}_{a_1^J} p_{\hat{\theta}}(s_1^J, a_1^J|t_1^I)$$

When estimating the parameters, the Expectation-Maximization (Dempster et al., 1977) algorithm is employed. In the E-step the counts for all the parameters are collected, and the counts are normalized in M-step. Figure 1 shows a high-level view of GIZA++.

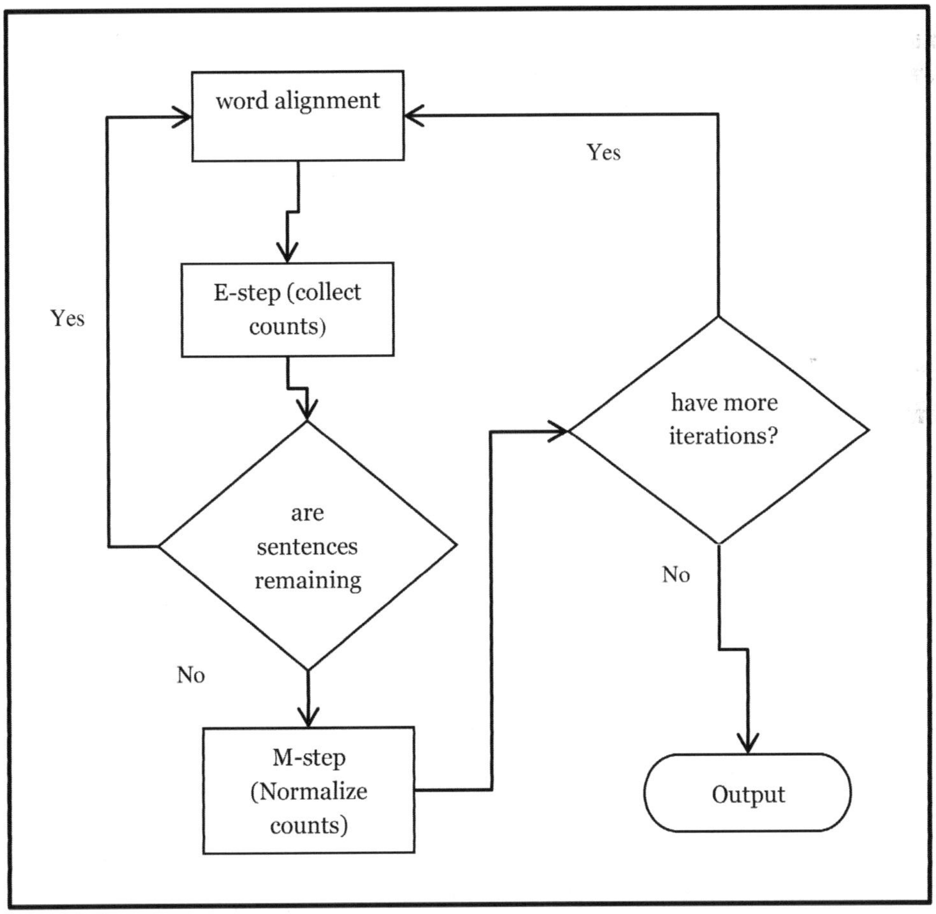

FIGURE 1 - GIZA++ algorithm overview

3 Distortion limit

Moses handles the reordering task using a reordering model (Koehn et al., 2003). This model is language independent and introduces a penalty when phrases are picked out of order. This penalty depends on the number of words skipped and is modeled by a linear distortion model given by

$$D(s,t) = p_f^1 + \sum_{i=2}^{P} d(i)$$

where P is the no. of phrases used to translate source s to target t, p_f^1 is the first word index of the source in first phrase and $d(i)$ is the distortion for phrase i given by

$$d(i) = |p_l^{i-1} + 1 - p_f^i|$$

where p_l^{i-1} is the last index of the source in previous phrase $i-1$ and p_f^i is the first index of the source in the current phrase i.

4 Phrase based model

Moses requires two types of data for training a phrase based model. Sentence aligned bilingual corpus to train the TM and the target side monolingual corpus for the LM. The TM presents itself in the form of a phrase-table which contains phrase entries and probabilities representing their mutual translation scores. The LM, however, represents the target language word order thereby ensuring good scores for a fluent output. A decoder component consults both the models to generate a sequence of phrases for a given test input.

In our experiment, we place this as a baseline system. Particularly, for the shared task data, the phrase based model has the following advantages:

- the same source and target language vocabulary can lead to a lesser sparse and improved translation model
- one to one mapping between source and target language words can result in a better alignment model

5 Factored model

Factored models are an extension of the phrase based models as they allow addition of factors to the training data. These factors could be linguistic annotations such as part-of-speech tags or any other relevant information used to improve the various models.
These factors are combined using a log-linear model given by the following equation.

$$p(t|s) = \frac{1}{Z} e^{\sum_{i=1}^{n} \lambda_i h_i(t,s)}$$

Each h_i is a feature function for a component of the translation and the values λ_i are the corresponding weights for the feature functions.
In the training data, each word is represented as a vector of factors, instead of a simple token. A phrase mapping is decomposed into several steps that either translate input factors to output factors or generate target factors to other target factors.

6 Experiments and results

The focus of this task as mentioned above is to learn the alignment information from the training data. Since the given data was in the CoNLL-X format, some preprocessing was done to obtain sentence aligned source and target data files for all language pairs. A distinct pair of source and target files was created for sentences containing indices, surface word forms and part-of-speech (POS) forms. In order to run trials on the phrase based and factored model, the data was split as per Table 1 below

	Numbers of sentences		
	English-Urdu	**English-Farsi**	**English-Italian**
Train	4500	3500	4500
Test	500	500	500
Development (Tuning)	500	500	500

TABLE 1 - Training, Testing and Development Data

A pair of trials was conducted with phrase based and factor based approach each with default parameters and tuned parameters.

The Moses default setting sets the distortion limit to 6. Therefore, if no. of words skipped is greater than 6 the translation will be pruned. This puts hard constraint and makes the model less suitable for more syntactically divergent languages like Urdu, Hindi, and Marathi etc. According to the choice of parameters, the correct reordering is sometimes improbable for large scale reordering. Thus, we have varied the distortion limits from 3 to 12 and observed the results for all trials.

Surface word form training was done for phrase based TM. We trained this baseline system with the original source sentences and the target reordered sentences.

For the factor based TM, we used a training data containing the surface form word and a POS tag (as an additional factor). Additionally, the training script included a mapping for translation-factors.

Translation-factor mapping:

[source side surface] to [target side surface + target side POS]

The format for factored model training data is as given below:

source format:
"a|DT developed|JJ pakistan|NN began|VBD taking|VBG shape|NN again|RB .|."

target format (reordered):
"a|DT developed|JJ pakistan|NN again|RB shape|NN taking|VBG began|VBD .|."

In terms of language model, surface word form LM was used for phrase based approach.

For the factored model, however, surface word form LM and POS based LM were used because better estimates of the target language order are provided by the POS LM. In comparison with the surface LM, the POS LM proves to be more useful on account of learning from a more generic target word order and richer evidences.

6.1 Experiments: without tuning

The results of the experiments on both approaches were evaluated for two test datasets. The first test dataset (test1) was obtained from splitting the provided data (ref. Table 1) and the second test dataset (test2) is the same on which the task results were announced. For BLEU evaluation and comparison, we requested the reference set for *test2* from the RSMT organizers. The results without tuning and with default parameter settings of Moses are shown in Table 2 below

	BLEU score phrase based model		**BLEU score factored model**	
	test1	**test2**	**test1**	**test2**
Urdu	42.59	42.21	44.54	44.07
Farsi	57.76	54.78	57.95	55.77
Italian	74.05	73.91	73.93	73.37

TABLE 2 - BLEU scores: default settings for phrase based and factored model

6.2 Experiments: with tuning

For tuning, the development data of 500 sentences was used. We evaluated results for varying distortion limit values after tuning. The motivation for this comes from the fact that the distance-based distortion model is placed as a weak model for highly divergent languages and our task is to learn reordering using alignments. Hence, the evaluation results might inform about the extent of reordering expected by each language pair.

	Urdu				**Farsi**				**Italian**			
Distortion limit	**Phrase based**		**Factored**		**Phrase based**		**Factored**		**Phrase based**		**Factored**	
	test1	**test2**	**test1**	**test2**	**test1**	**test2**	**test1**	**test2**	**test1**	**test2**	**test1**	**test2**
3	41.09	41.31	40.97	40.99	59.26	56.51	60.70	**57.89**	75.51	75.34	75.81	75.62
4	42.80	43.00	43.02	43.05	**59.67**	56.72	60.92	57.71	75.58	75.43	75.90	75.75
5	43.77	45.05	45.30	45.17	59.50	**56.87**	60.78	57.69	75.57	75.48	75.94	**75.80**
6 (def.)	44.32	45.12	45.96	45.58	59.51	56.76	61.05	57.55	**75.58**	**75.49**	75.94	75.78
7	45.38	45.60	47.26	46.36	59.56	56.71	**61.07**	57.78	**75.58**	**75.49**	75.94	75.78
8	45.67	45.98	47.51	46.97	59.56	56.74	**61.07**	57.66	**75.58**	75.47	75.94	75.76
9	**46.00**	**46.24**	**47.59**	47.97	59.51	56.64	60.98	57.48	75.56	75.44	**75.97**	75.74
10	45.40	45.76	46.94	**48.22**	59.05	56.35	60.70	57.38	75.46	75.30	75.96	75.63
11	45.23	45.64	46.49	47.95	58.68	55.83	60.39	57.17	75.21	75.00	75.79	75.18
12	44.85	44.78	46.05	47.74	57.78	54.93	60.03	56.51	74.80	74.49	75.45	74.75

TABLE 3-BLEU scores: after tuning and varying distortion limits

The evaluation results in the Table 3 for each pair of languages have been plotted below against varying distortion limit values. The dotted line in the plot represents phrase based values and the solid line represents the factor based values obtained after tuning. For a consistent comparison of the test results with that of the system, the scores obtained on the *test2* dataset are also plotted.

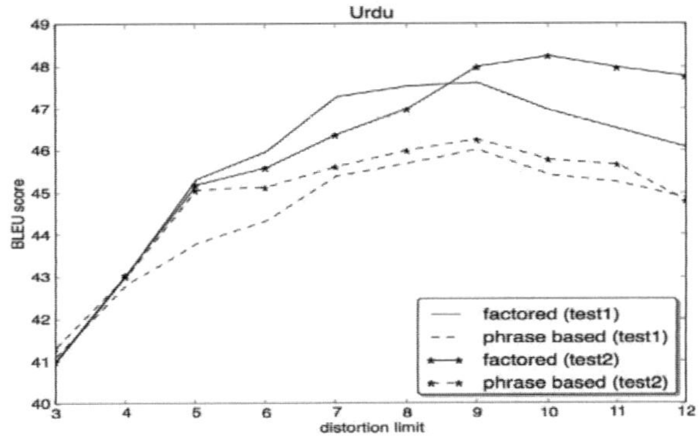

FIGURE 2 – BLEU score variation against distortion limit for Urdu

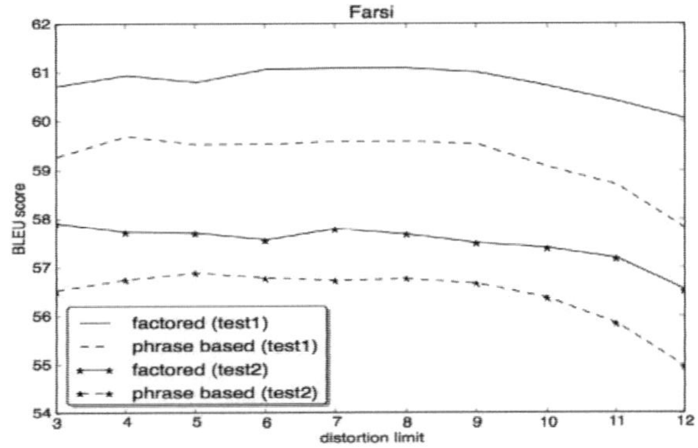

FIGURE 3 – BLEU score variation against distortion limit for Farsi

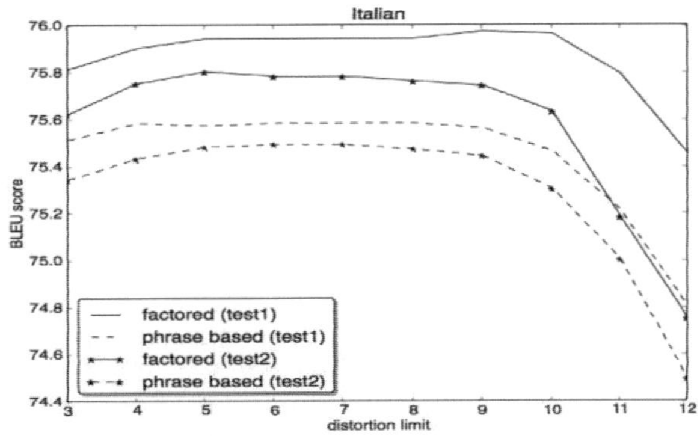

FIGURE 4 – BLEU score variation against distortion limit for Italian

6.3 Submission for the shared task

At the time of task submission the factored model with default settings was the best system we had. The mapping for translation factors was the same as described in Section 6. The system output for the test data provided by the organizers was obtained and eventually converted to the CoNLL-X format using some post-processing scripts. The results as provided by the organizers for the test corpus are given in the Table 4 below.

	Urdu	Farsi	Italian
BLEU score (our approach)	44.7	55.7	73.0
BLEU score (RSMT workshop baseline)	38.3	50.0	65.1

TABLE 4 - BLEU scores: test data results evaluated by the organizers

7 Conclusion and perspectives

With the default settings (before tuning) and for *test1*, factored model shows improvements for Urdu and Farsi pair only. However, English-Italian pair scores decrease slightly in the factored based approach. The same trend repeats for *test2* also. Apparently, the POS LM does not help the English-Italian pair with the default settings.

The Table 3 scores and graphs shown in Figure 2, 3 and 4 clearly show that the factored model (for *test1* and *test2*) outperforms the phrase based model for all languages after tuning is carried out. Although this varies for each language and the improvements are relatively high for Urdu and Farsi, only marginal improvements for Italian are observed.

More importantly, the plot for Urdu behaves sensitively for varying values of distortion limits. It begins to increase from a distortion limit value of 4 and attains a maximum at a value of 9 (for *test1*) and at 10 (for *test2*). The other languages do not vary highly against the distortion limit changes. Specifically, for *test2* the Urdu plot maintains good improvement even for distortion limit values of beyond 10. Evidently, this shows that Urdu prefers larger reordering and could be relatively more divergent.

The graphs also indicate a downward trend in scores for all languages from a distortion limit value of 10 onwards. The cause for this may be attributed to the increase in the number of translation choices during decoding, thereby increasing the error in selection of the correct hypotheses.

The plots for *test1* and *test2* follow the same trend in all cases except for Urdu factored, where BLEU score for *test2* does not drop heavily with increasing distortion limit values.

The results indicate that the shared task of learning reordering from the alignment information is modeled well by the approach as described above. This also resulted in improved BLEU scores over that of the baseline scores provided by RSMT.

References

Brown, P. F., Pietra, S. A. D., Pietra, V. J. D., and Mercer, R. L., (1993). The Mathematics of Statistical Machine Translation: Parameter Estimation. *Computational Linguistics*, 19(2):263-311

Dempster, A., Laird, N., and Rubin, D.,(1977).Maximum Likelihood From Incomplete Data via the EM Algorithm. *Journal of the Royal Statistical Society*, Series B, 39(1):138

Koehn, P., and Hoang, H., (2007). Factored Translation Models. *Proceedings of the 2007 Joint Conference on Empirical Methods in Natural Language Processing and Computational Natural Language Learning*, pp. 868–876, Prague, June 2007.

Koehn, P., Hoang, H.,Birch, A., Callison-Burch, C., Federico, M., Bertoldi, N., Cowan, B., Shen, W., Moran, C., Zens, R., Dyer, C., Bojar, O., Constantin, A., and Herbst, E., (2007). Moses: Open source toolkit for statistical machine translation. *In ACL*, Demonstration Session.

Koehn, P., Och, F. J., and Marcu, D.,(2003). Statistical phrase based translation. *In NAACL.*

Och, F. J., and Ney, H., (2003).A Systematic Comparison of Various Statistical Alignment Models, *Computational Linguistics*, volume 29, number 1, pp. 19-51 March 2003.

Papineni, K., Roukos, S., Ward, T., and Zhu, W., (2001). BLEU: a method for automatic evaluation of machine translation. *IBM Research Report*, Thomas J. Watson Research Center.

Vogel, S., NeyH., and Tillmann, C., (1996). HMM-based Word Alignment in Statistical Translation. *In COLING: The 16th International Conference on Computational Linguistics,* pp. 836-841, Copenhagen, Denmark.

Partially modelling word reordering as a sequence labelling problem

Anoop KUNCHUKUTTAN[1] *Pushpak BHATTACHARYYA*[1]
(1) IIT BOMBAY, Mumbai, India
anoopk@cse.iitb.ac.in, pb@cse.iitb.ac.in

ABSTRACT
Source side reordering has been shown to improve the performance of phrase based machine translation systems. In this work, we explore the learning of source side reordering given a training corpus of word aligned data. Given the large number of re-orderings this problem is NP-hard. We explore the possibility of representing the problem as a reordering of word sequences, instead of words. To this end, we propose a sequence labelling framework to identify work sequences. We also model the reversal of word sequences as a sequence labelling problem. These transformations reduce the problem to a phrase reordering problem, which has a smaller search space.

KEYWORDS: Statistical machine translation; Source reordering; Sequence labelling; Word alignment.

Proceedings of the Workshop on Reordering for Statistical Machine Translation, pages 47–54,
COLING 2012, Mumbai, December 2012.

1 Introduction

Phrase based machine translation is one of the most successful SMT paradigms in recent times. However, one of its major weaknesses has been the lack of a good distortion model, due to which reordering could not be handled correctly. Distance based penalty models would work only for language pairs where the word order is very similar. Practical constraints like the decoder's large search space also limit the possible reorderings that can be searched during decoding. Lexical binary reordering model (Koehn, 2008) proposes a limited reordering model conditioned on the phrases. An alternative approach which has been proposed is to reorder the source language sentence to conform to the target language word order before decoding. The search space for the decoder is thus simplified, and thus translation can be performed effectively with a simple distortion model. Many solutions for manipulating source side parse trees, with manual (Collins et al., 2005; Ananthakrishnan et al., 2008) or automatic rules (Xia and McCord, 2004), have shown improvement in the performance of PBSMT. However, these solutions are language pair specific, cannot be easily scaled to new language pairs and may require linguistic resources like parsers on the source/target sides.

Therefore, recently, approaches have been explored to learn word reorderings on the source side in a language independent way. Visweswariah et al. (2011) model the word reordering as a Travelling salesperson problem whereas Tromble and Eisner (2009) model it as a linear ordering problem. Given the large number of re-orderings this problem is NP-hard. We explore the possibility of representing the problem as a reordering of word sequences, instead of words. To this end, we propose a sequence labelling framework to identify work sequences. We also model the reversal of word sequences as a sequence labelling problem. These transformations reduce the problem to a phrase reordering problem, which has a smaller search space.

In Section 2, we discuss our word sequence based reordering model, and how it has been partially cast as a sequence labelling problem. Section 3 discusses our experiments. Section 4 describes the results of our experiments and analyses the results.

2 Reordering Model

2.1 Motivation

Visweswariah et al. (2011) and Tromble and Eisner (2009) have considered the source reordering problem to be a problem of learning word reordering from word-aligned data. Finding the right reordering is exponential in the number of words in the sentence and hence intractable. Use of heuristics to overcome this bottleneck will result in suboptimal solutions. However, a key observation that can be made is that word sequences, as opposed to individual words, are displaced from their original position. Another common transformation is that a sequence of words get reversed. As an example, in 1, we can see that the that are two word sequences. The second word sequence also undergoes reversal. Source side reordering can thus be considered to be a composition of the following operations on a sentence:

- Breaking the sentence into word sequences
- Reverse some of the word sequences
- Reorder the word sequences

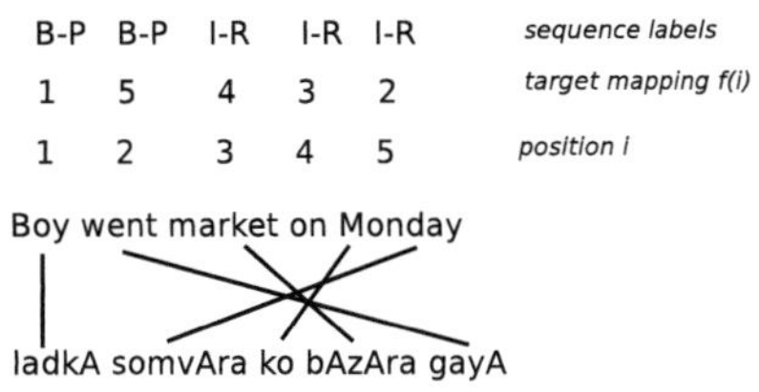

Figure 1: An example of word sequences and their sequence labelling

2.2 Sequence Labelling Model

We model the first two steps as a sequence labelling problem. For this purpose, we use a labelling scheme similar to the one used for sentence chunking. Our label set consists of two types of labels at the top level: beginning-of-word-sequence (B) and inside-word-sequence (I). There is only one type of B label (B-P), whereas there are two types of I labels:

- I-R: This indicates that the word is part of a word sequence which has been reversed.
- I-S: This indicates that the word is part of a word sequence which has not been reversed.

Figure 1 gives you an example of the sequence labels.

2.2.1 Generating training data

Here we describe a method to generate the label sequences from the word alignment information. Given the word alignment information, for every position i in a training data sentence, we can obtain its position in the reordered sentence $f(i)$. The beginning of a word sequence is indicated by the mismatch between i and $f(i)$, whereas within a word sequence we can label a word at position i as 'I-S' or 'I-R' depending on the whether $f(i)$ precedes or follows $f(i-1)$. Algorithm 1 describes our method to determine the label sequences given $f(i)$ for the training data.

2.3 Reordering the phrases

For reordering word sequences, we adapt the method of Visweswariah et al. (2011) to word sequences - where reordering is modeled as a Travelling Salesperson (TSP) problem. We consider word sequences, instead of words, to be the cities, and define the cost of travelling from one city to another. Since the cost is asymmetric, we convert the problem into a symmetric one by using the method suggested by Hornik and Hahsler (2009) of doubling the number of edges and setting weights appropriately . Finally, we use the Lin-Kernighan heuristic to solve the symmetric TSP problem tractably.

2.3.1 Generating training data

We model the cost between two word sequences, $c(w_i, w_j)$, as follows:

$$c(w_i, w_j) = |g(i) - g(j) - 1| \text{ if } g(i) < g(j) \quad (1)$$
$$= 2 * |g(i) - g(j) - 1| + 1 \text{ otherwise} \quad (2)$$

where,
i, j are source word sequence positions and $i < j$

Algorithm 1 Generating sequence labels from word alignments for training

```
                                              ▷ i: position i in source sentence
          ▷ f(i): position in target sentence of word at position i in source sentence
state ← 'start'
for i = 1 → len(sentence) do
    if state = 'in' then
        if f(i) = f(i−1) + 1 then
            label[i] ← 'I-S'
        else
            if f(i) = f(i−1) − 1 then
                label[i] ← 'I-R'
            else
                state ← 'start'
            end if
        end if
    end if
    if state = 'start' then
        label[i] ← 'B-P'
        state ← 'in'
    end if
end for
```

$i = 0$ represents a beginning-of-sentence marker
$g(k)$ is the position of the phrase sequence at position k after source reordering
The cost for the case $i > j$ can be obtained by symmetry from the above equation.

The intuition behind the cost assignment is that the cost is less if the words are closer to each other in the reordered sentence. In addition, if the positions of word sequences are reversed with respect to each other, it incurs an additional cost which is modelled by the multiplicative factor.

To illustrate this consider the following example with word sequences and their reorderings

I	walk	fast office	*sentence with word sequences*
1	2	3	*i - index of word sequence*
1	3	2	$g(i)$ *- index of word sequence after reordering*

The cost assignment between word sequences is shown in Figure 2:

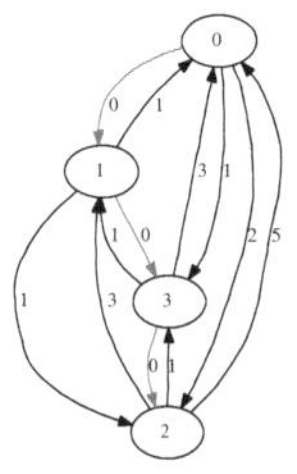

Figure 2: An example of cost assignment to phrase sequence orderings

2.4 Estimating cost between cities

The cost is defined as a function of the lexical and syntactic features as follows:

$$c(i,j) = \phi(s_i, s_j, (s))$$

where,
i, j are positions of the source side word sequences as identified by the sequence labeller (s) is the set of word sequences in the sentence

Our conjecture is that the reordering and the cost depends only the words at the ends of the word sequences under consideration. Hence for features we use information from the words at ends of the word sequences only.

ϕ is assumed to be a linear function of the features and the parameters are learnt using SVM regression.

However, for each sentence containing n word sequences, there will be $n(n+1)$ such cost instances. This results in a large number of training instances. Hence we train the regression model from the cost instance of a subset of the training sentences. However, we assume that this would not affect the accuracy of the regression model, since the same syntactic effects would be affecting the cost model across all the sentences in the same language pair.

3 Experiments

This section describes the dataset used and the sequence labelling, cost modelling and TSP experiments.

3.1 Data

Language Pair	Training	Dev	Test
en-fa	5000	500	500
en-ur	5000	500	500
en-it	4000	500	500

Table 1: Data set size

We experimented with word aligned data in three languages - English, Persian and Italian. The details of the dataset are summarized in Table 1. In addition to the word alignment information, coarse POS tag, fine POS tag and chunk information were used. The chunk information was obtained by flattening complete parse tree information available from a statistical parser.

3.2 Sequence Labelling

Sequence labelling was done using the *CRF++* toolkit. The sequence labels for training the CRF were obtained using the procedure mentioned in Algorithm 1 and all the training data was used for learning the CRF model. We experimented with binary features involving only the current label (unigram features) as well as current and previous label (bigram features). The entire list of features used is listed below:

Unigram features - $f(l_i, x)$, where x stands for one of

- Tokens at positions 0, 1, 2, -1 and -2 from current token.
- POS tags at positions 0, 1, 2, -1 and -2 from current token.
- Chunk tags at positions 0, 1, 2, -1 and -2 from current token.

Bigram features - $f(l_i, l_{i-1}, x)$, where x stands for one of

- Token at position 0 from current token.
- POS tag at position 0 from current token.
- Chunk tag at position 0 from current token.

Adjacent labels - $f(l_i, l_{i-1})$

where, l_k is label of position k in the sentence.

We experimented with different configurations of the above features and the best result was obtained when all the above mentioned features were used.

3.3 Cost Regression Model

The regression models were trained using the SVMLight (Joachims, 1999) implementation of SVM regression. An RBF kernel with default values for the parameters c and γ was used. Three cost regression models were build using subsets of the entire training set containing 500, 1000 and 1500 sentences respectively.

The following features were used for both the word sequences in each training instance :

- If the word sequence is reversed
- Token, POS and Chunk from positions 0 and 1 from the left end of the word sequence
- Token, POS and Chunk from positions 0 and 1 from the right end of the word sequence

4 Results and Analysis

Sequence Label	en-fa			en-ur			en-it		
	P	R	F-1	P	R	F-1	P	R	F-1
B-P	79.75	70.22	74.69	83.71	80.47	82.06	77.92	61.55	68.78
I-R	65.64	70.12	67.81	45.88	52.57	49.00	64.78	62.24	63.48
I-S	39.55	35.16	37.23	56.47	54.90	55.67	36.47	27.70	31.48

Table 2: Best sequence labelling results

Table 2 shows the per label accuracies of sequence labelling, for the best performing feature configuration (which is all the features listed in Section 3.2). Table 4 shows the monolingual BLEU scores for reordering. The scores are reported for three training configurations corresponding to the number of sentences used for training the cost estimation models. In all these cases, the best performing feature configuration for sequence labelling was used. The baseline comparison was the BLEU score on the original, unreordered sentences, which is shown in Table 3.

It is clear that the accuracy of sequence labelling is not good enough to predict the word sequence or sequence reversals. Especially, the accuracy in the prediction of sequence reversal is very low. This low level of accuracy of sequence labelling obviously makes it difficult to get good results with word sequence reordering. This is reflected in the low BLEU scores - which are near the baseline scores.

The use of a small subset for training the cost regression model does not result in significant deterioration of the BLEU score.

The low monolingual BLEU score could be attributed to the following reasons:

- The features used for sequence labelling are not sufficient to capture the phenomena of word sequence displacement and reversal.
- The choice of the cost model and features for regression
- About 10% of the TSP problems (with number of nodes < 8) were not solved by the Concorde solver.

Language Pair	BLEU
en-fa	51.36
en-ur	39.54
en-it	68.98

Table 3: Baseline Results (dev set)

Language Pair	500 sent	1000 sent	1500 sent
en-fa	49.14	49.2	49.1
en-ur	39.14	39.35	39.3
en-it	68.82	68.64	NA

Table 4: Evaluation results for different sizes of cost regression training data

Conclusion and perspectives

Although word sequence labelling is intuitively appealing, and the success of parser output based reordering rules suggests that phrase reordering is useful, the results presented have not been encouraging. However, we believe more work could be done in the following areas to improve the system:

- Choice of better features for the sequence labelling
- Better modeling of the cost between two word sequences
- Choice of better features for the cost regression model

References

Ananthakrishnan, R., Hegde, J., Bhattacharyya, P., and Sasikumar, M. (2008). Simple Syntactic and Morphological Processing Can Help English-Hindi Statistical Machine Translation. In *IJCNLP*.

Collins, M., Koehn, P., and Kučerová, I. (2005). Clause restructuring for statistical machine translation. In *Proceedings of the 43rd Annual Meeting on Association for Computational Linguistics - ACL '05*.

Hornik, K. and Hahsler, M. (2009). Tsp-infrastructure for the traveling salesperson problem. *Journal of Statistical Software, 23 (i02)*.

Joachims, T. (1999). Making large-Scale SVM Learning Practical. In *Advances in Kernel Methods - Support Vector Learning*.

Koehn, P. (2008). *Statistical Machine Translation*. Cambridge University Press.

Tromble, R. and Eisner, J. (2009). Learning linear ordering problems for better translation. In *Conference on Empirical Methods in Natural Language Processing*.

Visweswariah, K., Rajkumar, R., Gandhe, A., Ramanathan, A., and Navratil, J. (2011). A Word Reordering Model for Improved Machine Translation. In *Empirical Methods in Natural Language Processing*.

Xia, F. and McCord, M. (2004). Improving a statistical MT system with automatically learned rewrite patterns. In *Proceedings of the 20th International Conference on Computational Linguistics - COLING '04*.

Author Index